THE ACADEMIC LIBRARY AND ITS USERS

The academic library and its users

Peter Jordan

Gower

Published by
Gower Publishing Limited
Gower House
Croft Road
Aldershot
Hampshire GU11 3HR
England

Gower
Old Post Road
Brookfield
Vermont 05036
USA

Peter Jordan has asserted his right under the Copyright, Designs and Patents Act 1988 to be identified as the author of this work.

British Library Cataloguing in Publication Data
Jordan, Peter, 1936–
  The academic library and its users
  1. Academic libraries 2. Libraries and students 3. Libraries and scholars
  I. Title
  027.7

ISBN 0 566 07939 9

Library of Congress Cataloging-in-Publication Data
Jordan, Peter, 1936–
    The academic library and its users/Peter Jordan.
       p. cm.
    Includes index.
ISBN 0–566–07939–9
    1. Academic libraries–Great Britain. 2. Libraries and readers–
  Great Britain. I. Title.
Z675.U5J73 1998   IN PROCESS
027.7′0941–dc21
                                                          98–6703
                                                              CIP

Phototypeset in Palatino by Intype London Ltd and printed in Great Britain at the University Press, Cambridge

Contents

Preface

A few years ago I was asked to teach a course at Manchester
Metropolitan University on the academic library and its
community. I was unable to find texts which considered the
users' view at all satisfactorily. Most writings by librarians concentrate on listing what is on offer but rarely relate it to the
needs of academic staff and students which arise from the
demands being made of them in a rapidly changing environment.

Now that libraries can offer even more wonderful facilities
as they change from 'just in case' collection-building mode to
'just in time' access through information technology, it is more
important that their facilities and expertise are offered primarily
as solutions to problems which the users need to solve. This
book therefore concentrates initially on the environment of
higher and further education, on the terminology we employ
about users and how we find out about their needs. The rest of
the book examines the needs of the various groups of users
and the ways in which the library can respond. The last chapter
surveys the future, which is highly dependent on the success
librarians have in making their services as relevant as possible

to the needs of their communities. Never take your eyes off the user!

Peter Jordan

1 The academic environment

The present system of further and higher education in the UK dates from the Further and Higher Education Act 1992. This Act established the two Further Education Funding Councils, one for England and one for Wales, and similarly the two Higher Education Funding Councils. The 1988 Education Reform Act had removed polytechnics and certain other colleges of higher education from Local Education Authority control and the 1992 Act similarly made colleges, including sixth-form colleges, self-governing. The 'binary line' between universities and other higher education institutions was abolished. These institutions chose to call themselves universities and are now generally referred to as 'new universities'. Since many of the new universities were themselves the result of earlier amalgamations of institutions, some of which were well established, they had inherited substantial library collections, though the quality was variable.

The Robbins Report of 1963 reviewed the pattern of higher education in Great Britain and concluded that there was a huge pool of untapped ability in the population and, assuming 'as an axiom that courses of higher education should be available

1

for all those who are qualified by ability and attainment to pursue them and who wish to do so' (Committee on Higher Education 1963, p.8), recommended a massive expansion of higher education. As a result university status was granted to ten colleges of advanced technology.

At the time of the Robbins Report the higher education institutions consisted of the ancient universities of Oxford and Cambridge and, in Scotland, St Andrews, Glasgow, Aberdeen and Edinburgh, and the federation of colleges and schools forming the University of London, the older 'civic' universities founded in the nineteenth century or early twentieth century (Durham, Manchester, Birmingham, Liverpool, Leeds, Sheffield and Bristol) plus the University of Wales, also dating from the late nineteenth century. Lastly there were the newer 'civic' universities of Reading, Nottingham, Southampton, Hull, Exeter and Leicester. In the 1960s eight more 'plate-glass' universities were established at Keele, Sussex, Norwich, York, Canterbury, Colchester, Coventry and Lancaster. These institutions have now had time to develop collections, some of them extensive.

Currently the further education sector consists of three major types of institution: further education colleges, including specialist institutions such as colleges of art and design and colleges of agriculture and horticulture; tertiary colleges; and sixth-form colleges. The general further education colleges offer a broad range of courses and cater for students of all ages from 16 upwards. The majority of tertiary colleges are similar to general further education colleges. 'What perhaps most distinguishes them from the traditional general further education college is that the average age of their students is lower and the fact that they attach particular importance to the needs of the 16 to 19 age group' (Cantor, Roberts and Pratley 1995, p.4). In recent years the sixth-form colleges have broadened their intakes by the introduction of vocational and pre-vocational courses. There are also colleges described by the funding councils as 'designated institutions' – certain adult education colleges and specialist institutions such as the National Sea Training College, and there is a significant private or independent sector.

Library provision in the further education sector varies a

great deal, with some of the specialist colleges having extensive resources, but 'libraries are often a weak aspect of provision. Many are too small for the number of enrolled students, have insufficient study spaces and an inadequate or outdated book stock' (Further Education Funding Council 1995, p.32). The Kennedy Report (Kennedy 1997), published by the Further Education Funding Council, argues strongly for a system in which everyone should achieve qualifications at an advanced level – either two A levels, an Advanced General National Vocational Qualification or a National Vocational Qualification at level three. It also recommends that restrictions on eligibility should be removed and access funds in the college sector be increased significantly. The report has won 'tacit backing' (Baty 1997a, p.5) from the government and could mean increases in the number of further education students and more poorly qualified entrants. Both these changes will directly affect library services.

During the last few years we have witnessed unprecedented national interest in higher education libraries, culminating in the publication of the Follett Report (*Joint Funding Councils' Libraries Review Group: Report 1993*) and its supporting documents.

The Parry Report

The major report on libraries before 1993 was the Parry Report, perhaps most famous for its recommendation, rarely achieved, that not less than 6 per cent of a university's budget should be spent on the library. In its opening pages the report focuses upon users and their needs:

The prime obligation of a university library is to the members of the institution of which it forms a part. It has to satisfy the needs of the undergraduate and must also meet the requirements of the graduate student who is embarking on research, and the much more complex and exacting demands of the mature scholar. (University Grants Committee 1967, pp.4–5)

It goes on to discuss in some detail the needs of undergraduates, graduates and scholars. It drew, for example, on its own survey results and upon the Hale Report on university teaching methods to conclude that the need for students to read extensively on their own would increase. It demonstrated admirable empathy in understanding the information needs of new lecturers:

In the case of the young lecturer it is important that his research work be facilitated in every way. He is the least able to travel in search of his material, or to accumulate an expensive private collection. Secondly, a well-stocked library is a strong element in attracting new members to the university and in retaining those already there. Thirdly, an impressive collection of research material in any subject, displayed on open access, is an incentive to the young research worker to set and maintain his standards, and to perpetuate a tradition of scholarly excellence. (University Grants Committee 1967, p.13)

The Atkinson Report

Ratcliffe (1980, pp.1–2) has described the appearance of the Atkinson Report (University Grants Committee 1976) as seeming 'quite inexplicable in the light of the Parry Report . . . as pessimistic a document as the latter was optimistic'. It is chiefly remembered for its concept of the 'self-renewing' library 'in which new accessions would be relieved by the withdrawal of obsolete or unconsulted material'. Although there is an introductory statement about the need to support teaching and research, the recommendations arise from a variety of statistical and financial evidence, not from any discussion of users' needs. Consequently the note appended to the report from SCONUL (Standing Conference of National and University Libraries) heralded considerable debate about the effect on users if the 'self-renewing' concept were applied to all university libraries:

Reform in the content of the readily available stock can only be meaningful if it is in the context of academic programmes and rationalisation should originate from this area. Furthermore, it would be dangerous to group all stock within a single category using a single criterion for assessment: book and periodical use in the Humanities differs from such use in the Pure Sciences and differs even more greatly from use in the Applied Sciences. (University Grants Committee 1976, p.40)

The Follett Report

The Follett Report (*Joint Funding Councils' Libraries Review Group: Report 1993*) was undertaken at a time of great change in higher education which demanded 'a sea-change in the way institutions plan and provide for the information needs of those working within them' (*Joint Funding Councils' Libraries Review Group: Report 1993*, p.5). In particular the situation had changed since that of Parry who, for example, recommended that there should be a high percentage of research material immediately available in all subject fields, and Atkinson, who was so concerned about space requirements for increasing amounts of material, because of developments in information technology. The emphasis has shifted towards information and information access and away from holdings. 'This has profound and far reaching implications, and all institutions must act to ensure that they are in a position to deal with these to best advantage' (*Joint Funding Councils' Libraries Review Group: Report 1993*, p.5). In contrast to Atkinson, this report makes frequent reference to the needs of users, beginning with a statement that libraries will continue to play a central part in meeting the information needs of students, teachers and researchers. It acknowledges that developments in the organization of teaching and learning have increased demands on libraries and emphasizes the need for improvements in liaison between the library and teaching staff and in the recognition of the role of libraries in assessments of teaching quality.

The Follett Report lists some of the developments in higher education which are changing the environment for library and related provision (*Joint Funding Councils' Libraries Review Group: Report 1993*, pp.17–26). These developments, which are equally applicable to further education, are discussed in the rest of this chapter. Much of this book is devoted to a discussion of how libraries can respond effectively.

Recent developments

1.   Growth in student numbers
There was rapid growth in the late 1960s following the Robbins Report, a long pause throughout the 1970s and early 1980s, and then rapid growth again. Figures quoted in the Dearing Report (National Committee of Inquiry into Higher Education 1997, ch. 3) show that the number of students in higher education in the United Kingdom rose from 321,000 in 1962–63 to 671,000 in 1979–80 to 1,481,000 in 1995–96. In the early 1960s only one young person in eighteen entered full-time higher education in the United Kingdom. In 1997 the figure was nearer one in three, and around 45 per cent in Scotland and Northern Ireland. Of particular importance to libraries, it is postgraduate numbers that have grown fastest in recent years.

In further education in the United Kingdom there were 1,007,000 in 1970–71 and 2,494,000 in 1993–94 – an increase in 23 years of over almost 130 per cent (Great Britain. Statistical Office 1996).

2.   A decline in library expenditure
The amount spent per capita on libraries declined, as did the proportion of the institutional budget.

3.   Increased prices of books and periodicals
Between 1980–81 and 1991–92 the Blackwell's Periodicals price index rose by almost 300 per cent.

4.   Changes in the make-up of the student population
This has primarily taken the form of an increase in part-time and mature students. Dearing (National Committee of Inquiry into Higher Education 1997, pp.19–20) points out that the

balance between full- and part-time study has not changed significantly since the 1960s but the total number of part-time students in higher education in the United Kingdom has increased from 119,000 in 1962–63 to 447,000 in 1995–96 plus 112,000 Open University students. In addition:

In 1979–80 young students (those under the age of 21 on entry to an undergraduate programme, or under the age of 25 on entry to a postgraduate programme) were only just in the majority; by 1995–96, 58 per cent of entrants to higher education were mature. The majority of mature students study part-time. (National Committee of Inquiry into Higher Education 1997, p.21)

In further education the number of part-time students in the United Kingdom has increased from 905,000 in 1970–71 to 1,756,000 in 1993–94, though the proportion has decreased from 83 per cent to 70 per cent (Great Britain. Central Statistical Office 1996).

5. *Changes in course design*

Increasingly a systems approach to courses has been adopted, with written statements being required on their objectives, their content, methods of delivery, assessment of students and ways in which the course will be monitored and evaluated. These statements are invaluable to librarians supporting courses. Courses have also been made more flexible to give a greater choice to students. Commonly courses are divided into self-contained units or modules with students able to choose, within certain limits, the modules they wish to take. Since modules appear on a cyclical basis it is frequently the case that a large number of students wish to study a module at the same time, which does create difficulties for support services. The problem is compounded by the fact that modules are often quite short in duration. Liaison between the library and tutors is even more necessary than usual in these circumstances.

6.   *Changes in teaching and learning methods*

The learning environment of students to-day is quite unlike that
in the 1960s. The dramatic increase in student numbers, which
has not been matched by a proportionate increase in funding,
staffing or other resources, has resulted in increased class sizes,
decreased class contact time for students, and an increase in
students studying off campus. (National Committee of Inquiry
into Higher Education 1997, pp.34–5)

The Dearing Committee found that the teaching methods
experienced by most students were lectures, seminars and
tutorials, essays and projects and dissertations. They did,
however, find that teaching methods which had increased more
than 50 per cent over the last five years were interactive coursework, multimedia (use of videos increased by 47 per cent),
project work by students and team/group work by students.
  With the increase in student numbers and resource limitations, academic staff have sought to develop teaching methods
which remain effective but are less labour-intensive. Thus traditional lecturing has continued to occupy a prime position
since large numbers of students can be taught at one time.
There have been many criticisms, especially where the lecture
is misunderstood, where too much detail is attempted, and
because students mainly remain passive during the delivery.
Beard and Hartley (1984, p.156) have identified five styles of
lecturing, each of which leads to a variety of demands being
made on the library. The oral lecturer rarely uses any means of
communicating other than talk. To avoid misunderstanding and
to check on what has been heard, the conscientious student
must use the library extensively and may have difficulties if
sources receive only oral reference. In her survey of undergraduates, for example, Harrop (1981, p.3) found that the name
of an author recommended in a lecture was misspelt by five
out of seven students. Similarly, eclectic lecturers place demands
on students because they are unable to structure their presentations and tend to digress from the contents of their notes.
Amorphous lecturers, though confident, are ill prepared and

vague. It could be said that these three styles drive students to the library because of lecturers' failures and, since the library will contain the writings of experts in the subject, students may ultimately improve their learning.

Visual lecturers provide lots of visual information and give full notes visually to their students. Exemplary lecturers provide well-structured lectures that are not too detailed. They are more likely to provide handouts containing notes and further reading. Less conscientious students are likely to rely on notes to the exclusion of further reading, especially if it is known that good marks can be obtained without additional work. More conscientious students are likely to be motivated to add to the lecture notes through wider reading.

As Thrift (1995, p.389) has pointed out, 'what lecturers expect their students to read and what they actually read are two very different things', and the rewards they receive for 'wider reading' may not be what the students expect:

Peter has had to write several Economics essays for his tutor. For one he used two standard texts and two other books. He was, he said, 'a bit cheesed off' when he had the essay returned by his tutor with the comment 'You don't seem to have read very widely for this essay.' The next time he was set an essay he used only one book – 'the sort you buy at W. H. Smith to help you get through A level.' This time the tutor commented 'Good, you have obviously read more for this essay'. (Harrop 1981, p.2)

Students clearly learn from such experiences, which they relate to their fellow students.

Reading lists have always presented a problem for librarians even when there is a facility on the computer network because it is so difficult to extract them from lecturers:

Some more enlightened lecturers have dispensed with reading lists altogether, thereby encouraging students to do their own research. This has the effect of reducing the demand on any one particular title, journal article or case report, but in practice is not popular with students, particularly now that courses run for only half of the year, thus increasing demands on their time. (Thrift 1995, p.389)

Lectures delivered to large numbers of students are necessarily teacher-dominated but further and higher education more than ever is seeking to produce students who are active rather than passive and have developed a high level of communication skills. Macfarlane (1992, p.5) employs the term 'active learning' to emphasize 'the importance of ensuring that students engage actively in the learning process, rather than passively accept the work as a component of course requirements' and to describe the process in which 'students take more responsibility for their own learning . . . Active learners seek out the information they need, judge their own progress, and are group-motivated.' This approach clearly has implications for libraries which Macfarlane (1992, p.2) acknowledges:

Libraries are a vitally important part of all higher education institutions. In simplified terms, one of the key arguments which is developed in this report is that there will be a progressively increasing emphasis on, and provision for, self-paced teacher-supported individual learning. This implies an appropriate provision of supporting resources, available in a wide range of media and delivered by a variety of means. Library resources and functions would be key elements in providing the necessary learning support.

This emphasis can be supported by a reduction in the number of formal lectures, appropriate assessment systems in which projects and assessed coursework predominate and, more formally, by independent learning and 'learning contracts'. 'Learning contracts provide a vehicle for making the planning of learning experiences a mutual undertaking between a learner and his helper, mentor, teacher and often, peers' (Knowles 1990, p.213). An important stage in the negotiation of a learning contract is the identification of learning resources to support the contract and once the learner begins to carry out the contract he or she will be searching for information rather than following a prescribed reading list, and that has profound implications for academic libraries.

Active learning and the development of communication skills have been fostered through tutorials and discussion groups. The tutorial system has been the backbone of teaching in the older universities but it is very expensive if academic staff are to be present. Thus the use of collaborative student groups is seen as a way forward. Students can meet independently of the lecturer and work, for example, on a project which is presented orally and in written form to the tutor and may be peer-assessed. Discussion groups and tutorials of all types need adequate preparation if they are to work well, so the library is of increasing importance in the provision of information.

Macfarlane (1992) believes that information technology probably provides the greatest opportunity for further and higher education to improve standards, or even to cope with the expansion in student numbers and the increasing heterogeneity of students, by marrying the strengths of conventional teaching and the opportunities provided by the technology. The report reviews the current use of information technology in teaching and learning – computer-assisted learning systems, general tools such as word processing and the use of networks to send assignments to tutors, discipline-specific tools such as spreadsheets, computer-aided design and databases, simulations which represent the real world and the effect of changing the parameters, hypermedia, 'mind tools' which 'allow students to construct concept maps to explore their understanding of complex knowledge domains by producing interlinking patterns showing the nature of the relationships between concepts' (Macfarlane 1992, p.16). Learning can also be supported by using technology to facilitate communication – 'it is possible to create a cohort of students linked together, not only by face-to-face meetings, but by computer conferences which allow both synchronous and asynchronous communications' (Macfarlane 1992, p.16).

From security and access points of view much of this technology should be available in library and learning resource centres, and the library needs to be aware of developments in institutions. Dearing (National Committee of Inquiry into

Higher Education 1997, p.36) refers to the Teaching and Learning Technology Programme in which the funding bodies have invested £32 million to launch over 70 projects, though there is a shortage of staff skilled in developing computer-based course materials.

7.   Increasing focus on needs of users

More attention is now being given to the needs and perspectives of students as users of libraries, and on the library as a provider of a service. These are central concerns of quality management which is discussed in Chapter 2.

8.   Decline in students' book purchasing

This has been partly because of increases in book prices, but also because of changes in the student support system. Follett refers to the surveys undertaken by LISU – Library and Information Statistics Unit (*Joint Funding Councils' Libraries Review Group: Report 1993*, p.23) – which show that students in all subject areas are relying less on their own purchases. The recommendations of the Dearing Report and the Government's response (Baty 1997b, p.3) have made it clear that students will be relying more than ever on loans and will be less likely to purchase their own materials as public financial support decreases.

9.   Developments in information technology

Developments in IT are discussed throughout this book.

10.   New approaches to quality assessment and performance indicators

These are discussed in the next chapter.

References

Baty, Phil (1997a), 'The last shall be first', *Times Higher Education Supplement*, 1287, 4 July.

Baty, Phil (1997b), 'What Blunkett says . . .', *Times Higher Education Supplement*, 1290, 25 July.

Beard, Ruth M. and Hartley, James (1984), *Teaching and learning in higher education*, 4th edn, London: Harper and Row.

Cantor, Leonard, Roberts, Iolo and Pratley, Beryl (1995), *Guide to further education in England and Wales*, London: Cassell.

Committee on Higher Education (1963), *Higher Education Report of the Committee appointed by the Prime Minister under the chairmanship of Lord Robbins 1961–1963* (The Robbins Report), London: HMSO.

Further Education Funding Council (1995), *Quality and standards in further education in England: chief inspector's annual report 1993–94*, Coventry: Further Education Funding Council.

Great Britain. Central Statistical Office (1996), *Social Trends 26*, London: HMSO.

Harrop, Cherry (1981), 'The information needs of undergraduates project: some preliminary findings', *CRUS News*, 11, July.

Joint Funding Councils' Libraries Review Group: Report 1993 (The Follett Report), Bristol: Higher Education Funding Council for England.

Kennedy, Helena (1997), *Learning works: widening participation in further education*, Coventry: Further Education Funding Council.

Knowles, Malcolm (1990), *The adult learner: a neglected species*, 4th edn, Houston: Gulf.

MacFarlane, A. G. J. (1992), *Teaching and learning in an expanding higher education system*, Edinburgh: SCFC.

National Committee of Inquiry into Higher Education (1997), *Higher education in the learning society: report of the National Committee* (The Dearing Report), London: HMSO.

Ratcliffe, F. W. (1980), 'The growth of university library collections in the United Kingdom' in Thompson, James (ed.), *University library history: an international review*, London: Bingley.

Thrift, Heather (1995), 'Managing an academic law library: a personal view', *Law Librarian*, **26**(3), September.

University Grants Committee (1967), *Report of the committee on libraries* (The Parry Report), London, HMSO.

University Grants Committee (1976), *Capital provision for university libraries: report of a working party* (The Atkinson Report), London: HMSO.

2 Quality and the user

If quality did not exist, it would have to be invented to satisfy
a need. When you have decided what you are going to do
for clients, and how you are going to do it, there may be a
feeling that what is being done could be done better for them.
This feeling is about quality. (Whitehall 1992, p.23)

Quality is a positive concept and a most desirable characteristic
of any enterprise. It has been given special prominence since
the 1950s through the managerial strategies advocated by
American and Japanese gurus. For our purposes their emphasis
on customers makes their writings and their influence particularly appropriate for a book about users. In fact Feigenbaum
(1983) has defined quality as what the customer says it is and
Brophy, Coulling and Melling (1993, p.246), adapting the
concept to the current situation in academic libraries, define it
as 'the closest fit to users' needs that resources permit'. The
origin of the quality management movement lies in industry
where survival is frequently said to depend on producing
quality products. In further and higher education there has
increasingly been the 'need to acknowledge public account-

ability in respect of the use of public resources' (Rowley 1996, p.416) by providing proof of quality. The writers and practitioners of quality management agree on the necessity for a number of key features to be present if the aim of 'delighting the customer' (Melling 1996, p.28) is to be achieved.

First of all top management has to be committed. In total quality management it is seen as the main driving force – 'top management determines quality priorities, establishes the systems of quality management and the procedures to be followed, provides the resources, and leads by example' (Hill 1991, pp.541–68).

This commitment must be shared by all employees – 'all are responsible for ensuring quality in terms of "satisfying the customer" in all they do, and the approach is one of prevention of errors and faults rather than detection and correction' (Bendell 1991, p.2).

Customers and quality management

Quality management defines customers in a wider sense than normal. Each person or group in an organization responsible for a task which is then passed on to another employee or group must regard that person or group as customers, and a quality product must be provided for them. In libraries, for example, there are staff carrying out technical services functions such as acquisitions and database maintenance. Although they may not come into contact with users, they will be passing on their work to staff who will deal with users. Feigenbaum's ten crucial benchmarks aimed at making 'quality a way of totally focusing the company on the customer – whether it be the end user or the man or woman at the next work station or next desk' (Bendell 1991, p.16) epitomize the approach. Martin (1993, pp.38–45) is mindful of the problems should staff not be motivated by senior management, and also the difficulties of transferring industrial practices to libraries:

The difficulty of translating its [total quality management's] concepts into practice, the need for individual application of these concepts to the particular institution and the fact that most successful existing practice for comparison is in the manufacturing sector have presented severe stumbling blocks and led to what is sometimes known as TQP (total quality paralysis), where the commitment to TQM made at senior management level does not filter down through organisational practices. The TQM gurus – Deming, Crosby, Juran – have not made specific recommendations for libraries!

Many of the writers on quality management emphasize not only the need for awareness and motivation to be passed down to the rest of the staff by committed senior management, but also the importance of empowering staff to make decisions and take responsibility. This, of course, requires an appropriate management style, training and support and 'works best where it is part of a customer service strategy and where guidelines are set down for the degree of responsibility that employees can take' (Cook 1997, p.122).

The quality movement, therefore, has much to do with the currently fashionable customer care initiative employed by many industrial and service organizations. One of the most influential pieces of research on the delivery of quality service focused on the perceptions and expectations of customers and on the dimensions of service which customers employ in evaluating service quality (Zeithaml, Parasuraman and Berry 1990, p.26):

Tangibles:	Appearance of physical facilities, equipment, personnel, and communication materials
Reliability:	Ability to perform the promised service dependably and accurately
Responsiveness:	Willingness to help customers and provide prompt service
Assurance:	Knowledge and courtesy of employees and their ability to convey trust and confidence

Empathy: Caring, individualized attention the firm pro-
                  vides its customers

The researchers went on to apply these criteria in surveys of
customers, managers and staff who had contact with customers.
Comparisons of managers' and contact personnel's responses
were made with those of customers' responses revealing a
number of significant gaps. This information was then used to
identify factors which caused the gaps and to which attention
needs to be paid if customer service is to improve. This analysis
is especially valuable for service organizations such as libraries
as it can be applied with benefit to individual organizations
seeking to improve their performance. The first gap was
between customers' expectations and management's perceptions of those expectations and factors responsible were
inadequate upward communication from contact personnel to
management, too many levels of management separating top
managers from contact personnel, and lack of marketing
research orientation. Methods of finding out about users and
marketing will be discussed in Chapters 3 and 8.

Staffing structures

The first two factors relate to staffing structures and communication channels. Bluck's researches (Bluck 1994, pp.224–42)
found some innovation in former polytechnics but pre-1992
university libraries seemed more rigid, with mainly hierarchical
and pyramidal structures whilst Crist (1994, p.47) takes the view
that

library organizations often reflect structures from the last century.
Staff who have selected their roles to emphasize passive service
feel themselves devalued as constrained budgets mean staffs are
downsized and technology seems to threaten basic service skills.

Bluck and Crist are particularly interested in team systems
which, with convergence of library and computing services and

the development of subject librarianship (discussed in Chapter 5) can be seen as the main structural developments in academic librarianship over the last ten to twenty years.

Bluck (1996, pp.87–104) uses Adair's definition of a team as 'a group in which the individuals have a common aim and in which the jobs and skills of each member fit in with those of others' (Adair 1987, p.95). Given the nature of academic librarianship, especially in multi-site operations, it is difficult, using this definition, to envisage sections and sites not operating as teams aiming to provide a service together. When libraries such as the University of Northumbria, Aston University and Queen's University of Belfast use the term, however, there is added value. A participative style of management is envisaged with team meetings 'the bedrock of the formal communication system' (Bluck 1994, p.231) and, though a hierarchical structure may remain, everyone is expected to make a contribution in decision making and, wherever possible, staff are empowered to take decisions themselves. In this book there is a particular interest in such developments because most team systems see improved service to users, internal and external, as a major aim, with those closest to users setting their own goals and priorities but following a total organization aim of providing quality service to users. 'Research at Northumbria showed a strong feeling among staff that teams help them to provide better services to users, encourage them to put users first, and help individuals to work effectively and to adapt to change' (Bluck 1996, p.97), and the positive results achieved through total quality management at Queen's University of Belfast are said to be 'created by people, working in teams with other people, with the aim of achieving the highest level of service for the people who form their customer base' (Butterwick 1993, p.31).

The way the library is structured matters little to users, but as they increasingly require access to information irrespective of format it does make sense for this to be reflected in the structure. Williams (1994, p.65) summarizes Royan's survey of 1993 which showed a range of responses to the development of IT from voluntary cooperation between service heads to a variety of merged departments, the most popular being the library merged with academic computing and media services. Both the Fielden (John Fielden Consultancy 1993) and Follett (*Joint Funding Councils' Libraries Review Group: Report 1993*) Reports considered the question of convergence and concluded that there was no one best method but that it was an organizational issue that should be addressed when developing an overall information strategy. Apart from financial considerations, the catalyst has been the growing interdependence of the services brought about by IT developments and the consequent similarities between the tasks performed by library staff and by computing staff:

> Both are increasingly spending their time assisting staff and students to make effective use of the potential of information technology. Library staff may be more concerned with how to access electronically-stored information which a few years before would only have been available in book or journal form, while computing staff are more concerned with the use of programmes which facilitate the production and manipulation of information, but the distinction is not important to the users of these services, who look for prompt assistance across the range of uses of information technology. (Williams 1994, p.55)

It is worth noting that restructuring will not necessarily produce improved services, especially if commitment is lacking and insufficient training and guidance is given to staff, and it should not be assumed 'there is a best way to manage (and that is team-based, flexible and flatter) . . . in de-centralised structures management can spend too much time ensuring their beloved structure is working (the teams are talking and so on) and not enough time ensuring the service is being delivered' (Munro 1996, p.37).

Customer expectations

The second gap identified by Zeitaml and colleagues was the discrepancy between management's perceptions of customers' expectations and service quality specifications. One factor considered responsible for this gap was inadequate management commitment to service quality, which has already been discussed. A second will be familiar to academic librarians – the perception of unfeasibility which is described as 'a managerial mind-set that may or may not be related to actual constraints on the organization' – 'an excuse for maintaining the status quo' (Zeithaml, Parasuraman and Berry 1990, p.77). In a rapidly changing environment libraries should be constantly reviewing services and procedures, but there can be a conflict when staff are perceived to be sticking too rigidly to rules and regulations. The rules are meant to provide a fair and equal service to everyone, though some groups may justifiably be given some preferential treatment, and if the rules are too vague and/or they are continually broken, the situation can become chaotic. A library in which some staff operate rules differently from others is not to the ultimate good of anybody. Having said this, there may be occasions when it is justified to break a rule, but when this happens it is often necessary to make it clear that a special exception is being made and perhaps a more senior member of staff should approve the action (taking into account what has already been written about empowerment).

Standardization of tasks

A further factor was the standardization of tasks which, largely through technology, has allowed more time to be spent on helping users. Experiments taking place under the Electronic Libraries Programmme in Britain are designed to make use of this facility. For example the Newcastle Electronic Reference Desk, which consists of a database of frequently asked questions and the answers which can be accessed by electronic mail

(McNab and Winship 1996, p.637). The prospect of increased professional help for users in academic libraries remains a distant one as many libraries have chosen to substitute professional by non-professional staff.

Prima facie this is unexpected since automation has saved unskilled work rather than professional. Demands for professional expertise have increased rather than decreased. The most likely explanation is that, in a period of budgetary constraint and burgeoning student numbers, accent has to be on the basic shelving and issuing functions at the expense of quality and technical service. (Sumsion 1994, p.120)

Service quality

The third gap is the discrepancy between service quality specification and actual delivery service, and this is seen to be caused by poor staff management including role ambiguity, role conflict, poor supervision and lack of teamwork.

The fourth gap was the discrepancy between actual service delivery and what is communicated to customers about it. The factors responsible were inadequate horizontal communications with, for example, advertisers and marketing and the propensity to overpromise. The publicizing and promotion of the library is discussed in Chapter 8.

A number of academic libraries have sought to publicize their quality aspirations by producing customer charters following the lead given by John Major when he launched The Citizen's Charter: raising the standard (1991). The six Charter principles which have guided public services developing charters of their own are listed by Payne (1996, p.73):

1. *Standards.* Publication of the standards of service that the customer can reasonably expect, and of performance against those standards.
2. *Choice and consultation.* Evidence that the views of those who use the service have been taken into account in setting standards.

3. *Information and openness.* Clear information about the range of services provided in plain language.
4. *Courtesy and helpfulness.* Courteous and efficient customer service from staff who are normally prepared to identify themselves by name.
5. *Putting things right.* Well-signposted avenues for complaint if the customer is not satisfied, with some means of independent review if possible.
6. *Value for money.* Independent validation of performance against standards and a clear commitment to improving value for money.

These principles are reflected in the charters produced by academic institutions and academic libraries. A Charter for Higher Education and a Charter for Further Education were issued in 1993 by the Department for Education. The former mentions libraries only once – 'Universities and colleges should ... explain the teaching and learning facilities available including libraries, information technology and other resources' (Department for Education 1993, p.13). The first academic library to be awarded a charter mark was Newcastle University Library in 1995 ('First academic charter mark awarded' 1996, p.6). A very good example of a published charter statement is Sheffield Hallam University Library and Learning Resources' 'Partnership in Learning', which opens with a statement of commitments:

- Providing services which meet the needs of all students based in the University, in accordance with University policy on equality of opportunity and within available resources;
- working with colleagues in Schools to ensure that library services are planned to meet the needs of students;
- guaranteeing confidentiality of personal information;
- providing high quality services through well trained staff;
- providing books, journals, audio-visual materials and electronic sources of information to support the curriculum;

- securing feedback from students;
- providing services at minimum costs to students.

These general commitments are then translated into statements of good practice as they relate to specific aspects of the service. Some are written in general terms, such as having opening hours that meet the needs of students, whilst others are more specific, such as a commitment to respond to 75 per cent of enquiries immediately, and dealing with specialist enquiries requiring referral within three working days.

The Sheffield Charter is a very similar document to the service level agreements which have become popular as 'contracts' between the library and academic departments. Revill and Ford (1994) have gathered together a number of university agreements and written a valuable introduction pointing out some of the problems involved. So far the responsibility of setting standards has lain with the provider but, as with many management techniques, it is best to get in first because 'if librarians do not originate them then someone else might and thereby produce a far less acceptable and less operable result' (Revill and Ford 1994, p.4).

It remains to be seen whether charters and service level agreements represent a passing fashion associated with the process of managerialism in the public services though, as (Payne 1996, p.84) points out 'the principles of consulting customers, setting out service standards and then reporting on performance are unlikely to go away'.

Performance indicators

Over the last decade or so a great deal of thought has been given to the most appropriate performance indicators for academic libraries. Winkworth (1993, pp.17–33) has neatly summarized efforts which have been made up to the early 1990s. This work has since been drawn upon first by Follett (*Joint Funding Councils' Libraries Review Group: Report 1993*, pp.31–3 and pp.81–2) and then in a consultative report by the Joint Funding Councils' Ad-hoc Group on Performance Indicators for Libraries (1995). Kinnell (1997, p.109) notes that a recent survey showed around 44 per cent of academic and industrial services were using performance indicators compared with over 80 per cent of public libraries.

Performance indicators are an essential part of quality control. Follett and the Ad-hoc Group use a framework comprising five areas to indicate overall library effectiveness: integration, quality of service, delivery, efficiency and economy. The last three are mostly concerned with statistics which measure performance of services (for example, number of documents delivered per full-time education (FTE) student during a year) or the underpinning necessary if service to users is to be effective (for example, total library expenditure per FTE student).

Following the award of a charter mark to Newcastle University Library, Morrow commented that 'a member of the public is not likely to be interested in how many books we process, but if he knows we can guarantee to get a certain book within as short a timescale as possible, that is more impressive' ('First academic charter mark awarded' 1996, p.6). It therefore has seemed more appropriate in this book to concentrate on those performance indicators directly concerned with quality of service to users which are necessarily more difficult to quantify. The first two categories in the framework are most relevant and are the concerns of the chapters which follow. For the integration category the Joint Funding Councils' Ad-hoc Group on Performance Indicators for Libraries (1995, p.9) recommend five performance indicators, all of which are especially relevant to the theme of this book:

1. The cohesiveness between the mission, aims, objectives and strategic plan of the institution and those of its library.
2. The resourcing mechanisms used by the institution to provide its library service.
3. The academic and research planning processes and outcomes.

4. Liaison between service providers and users.
5. Internal assessment and audit mechanisms.

The performance indicators for quality of service (termed 'user satisfaction' by the Ad-hoc Group) are concerned with the various services and the way in which knowledge of users' perspectives is obtained. Many of the recommended methods are discussed in Chapter 3.

Quality assessment in higher and further education

Both the UK Higher and Further Education Funding Councils have taken quality assessment seriously since they were set up. Following a review of initial procedures, the HEFC Quality Assessment Division revised its system in 1995. The Division concentrates on the assessment of subject areas and a number are chosen each year and assessed at each institution where that subject is taught. All institutions are visited and six aspects are assessed. Each is awarded a mark out of 4, giving a maximum of 24. Should a grade 1 (low) be awarded for any aspect it is subject to reassessment within a year. Naturally institutions are anxious to obtain high scores which can be publicized to attract students and quality staff. The six aspects under review are:

1. Curriculum design
2. Organization and content
3. Teaching, learning and assessment
4. Student achievement and progression
5. Student support and guidance
6. Learning resources and quality assurance and enhancement.

Clearly the last aspect is of most concern to the library, and the librarian should make every effort to ensure that accurate documentation is provided on the library's performance in that subject area. Attempts to reduce documentation to improve efficiency have tended to restrict the amount required from the library, which can even be ignored. It is also necessary for the library to make certain it is fully informed about the visit and that it is properly prepared, even though previous visiting parties may have largely ignored the library.

Assessments of institutions as a whole are also carried out. These are the quality audits conducted by the Higher Education Quality Council which reviews procedures, processes and mechanisms for maintaining and enhancing the quality of provision. In particular, validation, review, monitoring and evaluation of courses are covered. Once again it is imperative for the library to be involved in the preparation for the visit and for the visit itself.

Staff in the service departments should have a clear awareness of the institutional mission statement, corporate plan and strategic plan. The services should clearly be able to show how they fit into this plan and how they derive their quality assurance measures from it and support it. The interaction needs to be two way, not only are the services aware of the institutional context but the institutional plan takes into itself the services plan. (Harrison 1994, p.6)

The two forms of assessments of subject areas and institutional audit are to be made the responsibility of a single body, the Quality Assurance Agency, though assessment in Scotland remains with the Scottish Higher Education Council.

Institutions are also inspected by the professional and statutory bodies charged with accrediting the courses/programmes in particular vocational/professional subject areas. Sometimes inspections are combined with those of the funding councils.

My own experience supports the conclusion reached by the Follett Report that 'there has been relatively little explicit attention given to the contribution of library and related services to maintaining and improving the quality of teaching and learning by either of the quality bodies' (*Joint Funding Councils' Library Review: Report 1993*, paras 186–8). Davies (1994), who attended a training programme organized by the Further Education Funding Council (England) for occasional inspectors, also concluded that 'libraries and learning resource centres were not adequately dealt with' (p.4).

A natural reaction, whatever the activity, seems to be a perception that there is a lack of acknowledgement and appreciation of its true worth. A notable example is the treatment of 'support services', frequently viewed negatively as 'non-teaching' or 'non-academic' elements rather than integral parts of the academic enterprise. Consequently, as Jordan (1992) has shown, the reorganization of higher education in the late 1980s and early 1990s left many libraries underrepresented on internal groups responsible for the allocation of resources:

The consequences of changes like these for the library are such that ways of working need to be adjusted if the influence that was previously possible is to continue. Formal activity has to be replaced by an increase in informal activity such as casual meetings in dining rooms and coffee breaks and more frequent visits to departments to cultivate relationships. (Jordan 1992, pp.104–5).

Whatever we may think about the way in which some institutions have climbed on the quality bandwagon, few would quarrel with attempts to improve services to users and this remains a central tenet of quality approaches. Thus, as we have seen, customer care, appropriate staffing structures, attention to performance indicators, which tell us how we are serving users, and determination that the quality of service should be taken into account in formal quality assessments and audits, are all vital components.

References

Adair, J. (1987), *Effective teambuilding*, London: Pan.

Bendell, Tony (1991), *The quality gurus*, London: Department of Trade and Industry.

Bluck, Robert (1994), 'Team management and academic libraries: a case study at the University of Northumbria', *British Journal of Academic Librarianship*, **9**(3).

Bluck, Robert (1996), 'Organising libraries for customers' in Pinder, Chris and Melling, Maxine (eds), *Providing customer-oriented services in academic libraries*, Library Assocation.

Brophy, Peter, Coulling, Kate and Melling, Maxine (1993), 'Quality management: a university approach', *Aslib Information*, **21**(6), June.

Butterwick, Nigel B. (1993), 'Total quality management in the university library', *Library Management*, **14**(3).

The Citizen's Charter: raising the standard (1991), presented to Parliament by the Prime Minister, Cmnd 1599, London: HMSO.

Cook, Sarah (1997), *Customer care*, 2nd edn, London: Kogan Page.

Crist, Margo (1994), 'Structuring the academic library organization of the future: some new paradigms', *Journal of Library Administration*, **20**(2).

Davies, Jim (1994), 'The FEFC(E) inspectorate, quality considerations and college libraries and learning resource centres', *COFHE Bulletin*, 72, Summer.

Department for Education (1993), *The charter for higher education*, London: Department for Education.

Feigenbaum, A. V. (1983), *Total quality control*, New York: McGraw-Hill.

'First academic charter mark awarded' (1996), *Library Association Record*, **98**(1), January.

Harrison, Colin (1994), 'Anglia Polytechnic University draft working paper: preparing for quality audit', *COFHE Bulletin*, 72, Summer.

Hill, Stephen (1991), 'Why quality circles failed but total quality management might succeed', *British Journal of Industrial Relations*, **29**(4), December.

John Fielden Consultancy (1993), *Supporting expansion: a report on human resource management in academic libraries for the Joint Funding Councils' Libraries Review Group*, Bristol: Higher Education Funding Council for England.

Joint Funding Councils' Ad-hoc Group on Performance Indicators for Libraries (1995), *The effective academic library: a framework for evaluating the performance of UK academic libraries*, Bristol: HEFC.

Joint Funding Councils' Libraries Review Group: Report 1993, Bristol: Higher Education Funding Council for England.

Jordan, Peter (1992), 'Intra-institutional relationships', *British Journal of Academic Librarianship*, **7**(2).

Kinnell, Margaret (1997), 'Quality: is it just a management fad?', *Assistant Librarian*, **90**(7), July/August.

McNab, Alison and Winship, Ian (1996), 'Internet use in academic libraries', *Library Association Record*, **98**(12), December.

Martin, Di (1993), 'Academic libraries' in *Total quality management: the information business*, Hatfield: University of Hertfordshire.

Melling, Maxine (1996), 'Defining the customer's requirements for quality' in Pinder, Chris and Melling, Maxine (eds), *Providing customer-oriented services in academic libraries*, London: Library Association.

Munro, Julia (1996), 'Structures of the future seminar (SCONUL), 29–30 January 1996', *SCONUL Newsletter*, 7, Spring.

Payne, Philip (1996), 'User empowerment' in Pinder, Chris and Melling, Maxine (eds), *Providing customer-oriented services in academic libraries*, London: Library Association.

Revill, Don and Ford, Geoff (eds) (1994), *Working papers on service level agreements*, London: SCONUL.

Rowley, Jennifer (1996), 'New perspectives on service quality', *Library Association Record*, **98**(8), August.

Sumsion, John (1994), *Survey of resources and uses in higher education libraries: UK*, 1993, Loughborough: Library and Information Statistics Unit.

Whitehall, Tom (1992), 'Quality and information service: a review', *Library Management*, **13**(5).

Williams, A. G. (1994), 'Where are we going? The development of convergence between university libraries and computing services' in Harris, Colin (ed.), *New university library: issues for the '90s and beyond*, London: Taylor Graham.

Winkworth, Ian R. (1993), 'Into the House of Mirrors: performance measurement in academic libraries', *British Journal of Academic Librarianship*, 8(1).

Zeithaml, Valarie A., Parasuraman, A. and Berry, Leonard L. (1990), *Delivering quality service: balancing customer perceptions and expectations*, London: Collier Macmillan.

3 Users

'I do not want to go into the history of ignoring users, since there is not enough time to give an account of librarianship from its beginnings, even in summary.' Maurice Line's statement (Line 1981, pp.80–8) might come as a shock to some librarians who entered the profession because of its service orientation and lack of profit motive, but when they have thought about it many agree there is some truth in it. In particular senior managers who have limited direct contact with users and are faced with difficult resource decisions can easily be more influenced by the effect of decisions on themselves and their staffs than upon users. It is not unusual for library assistants and para-professionals to appear more concerned with service to users than their professional colleagues and

it is often the library assistants who act as the public side of the service and it is they who are the librarians in the eyes of many readers. Experience has often shown that the hesitant user in particular will often prefer to ask a library assistant the question rather than show his or her ignorance in front of an awe-inspiring professional. (Baker 1986, p.26)

The managerialist approach to public services which has been evident in the last decade has brought with it contrasting and often conflicting messages about users. On the one hand the language and practices of the business world can seem far removed from users as corporate plans, appraisal systems, compulsory competitive tendering, short-term contracts and suchlike take up so much staff time. On the other hand businesses are concerned with selling their products and therefore customers are important. Hence the interest in quality and customer consultation discussed in the last chapter.

There is a view that effective service to users ultimately means that each user should be dealt with as an individual and his or her needs met as far as possible. Carried to extremes this approach can cause considerable difficulties, especially where overall policies, designed to provide a service which is fair to everyone, are ignored. We have all encountered staff who let users off fines or allow them to borrow more items than the rules permit. Associated with this view is often a deep suspicion of generalizations which seem to subordinate individual behaviour to group norms. Studies of a group such as part-time students may show that they make little use of facilities provided at weekends, and policies may be formed with this information in mind. The knowledge that one part-timer does use weekend facilities does not invalidate the general finding, nor does it mean that the policy is wrong.

This discussion has already indicated a need for a structured, conceptual approach which will enable helpful consideration of 'user needs' to take place. Words such as 'need' and 'use' have been employed and often they lack the precision necessary to ensure productive dialogue. Line was aware of this difficulty when he produced his 'Draft definitions' (Line 1974, p.87) and these have been further developed by Green (1990, pp.65–78). I have drawn on the ideas of both these writers in what follows.

Terminology

'Need' is generally thought to be the superior concept which is informed by the other concepts because it is what a person ought to have to meet a goal. In the context of a library user we shall normally be referring to a need for information, though other needs may readily spring to mind, such as the need to have rules and regulations which control use of the library. The punishment to be meted out to students who steal or vandalize library materials is a frequent topic amongst academic librarians. The major problem with 'need' is who decides it. The users may be unaware of their real needs because they lack knowledge and are therefore unable to articulate them satisfactorily. Because of a natural wish to help, they will also frequently not say specifically what they want. Thus a person may ask where the economics books are rather than requesting a source which will provide information on the life of Keynes, and they may also be unaware that a biographical dictionary would be a better source. As Green points out, needs are therefore contestable, and most professionals would take the view that their superior knowledge and skill place them in the best position to assess and determine need. Professional librarians will undoubtedly be more familiar with the tools produced by themselves and other librarians such as catalogues, bibliographies and online searching facilities, which will often be the instruments best suited to obtaining the information required. Professionals naturally value their own expertise as it serves to validate their position and status. Cynics might add that some professionals produce tools which only they can understand, and demystification is needed to make tools more user-friendly. The debate about the role of the librarian as an intermediary and system navigator, which will be explored later, illustrates these points very well.

Green also points out two other reasons why we should not accept the verdict of the professional too readily. For one thing the academic librarians have to operate 'within the context of an ever tighter apparatus of power, within and outside the institution, that increasingly lays down itself what needs staff and students will have' (Green 1990, p.69), and they cannot therefore be seen simply as free agents making their own professional decisions. Additionally there is increasing scepticism about professionals with the media frequently publicizing the mistakes of doctors, teachers, architects, lawyers and social workers, among others.

'Need' should be the superior concept because it 'emphasizes above all the people for whom the library exists: its users' (Green 1990, p.75). The job of the professional is to build up a picture of need 'from a comprehensive examination of all the actors in a need situation' (Green 1990, p.72). The information gathered from the user will normally be at the first point of contact, and this will often take the form of a 'want' – 'what an individual would like to have' (Line 1974, p.87). A want becomes manifest when the user expresses it as a 'demand' by making a request. This demand has to be considered in the context of the institution's policy and the learning situation of the enquirer. For example, a request may be made for a piece of information which the user ought to find for him/herself. The policy of the institution is that students should be taught how to find information as part of their education and the student's tutor also wants the students to find information rather than have it spoon-fed to them. For such a request to be dealt with satisfactorily requires interpersonal skill on the part of the librarian, an understanding of the educational objectives of courses, and well-developed communication between course providers and librarians. Much of this book will be devoted to demonstrating how this can be achieved.

'Use' has been defined as 'what an individual actually uses' (Line 1974, p.87) and can provide valuable information for the librarian in deciding on policy and assembling sources of information. Of course individuals can only use what is available and they are constrained by what they know and how much effort they are prepared to make. For example, users may be unwilling to travel to obtain material they really want, and are prepared to use a substitute which requires less effort on their part. The fact that a substitute offered by a librarian, knowledgeable about the student's needs and about the stock of the library, could well prove more helpful does show how difficult it is to make certain inferences from statistics of use.

The social action approach

Because libraries exist for users, it is the user who should be at the centre of concerns. The social action approach, identified by sociologists, has much to offer because it starts with the individual and the meaning he/she attaches to his/her behaviour. 'To explain an action is, for the most part, to understand the position of an actor in a particular situation or type of situation' (Cohen 1968, p.73). Further,

The actions of men are governed not simply by the circumstances of situations which are external to them, but also by the subjective manner in which these situations are experienced. The subjective elements in situations are the actor's ideas, feelings and state of knowledge. These elements are very often culturally shared. (Cohen 1968, p.74)

Service providers who do not recognize such an approach are more likely to see situations from their own viewpoint. At the extreme, librarians have been known to think of users as nuisances who prevent them getting on with what they perceive as their real work. On the other hand those taking a social action approach try to understand the meanings which users attach to their situations. For example, how does a new student feel about entering a large academic library for the first time? How can we explain the behaviour of such students when it can appear 'stupid' to the trained librarian. 'You attended the induction talk so you should be able to find the information yourself!'

Key concepts

There are a number of key concepts used by sociologists which can help in the analysis of situations involving users. 'Norms' are behaviours, attitudes, opinions or perceptions which conform with what is acceptable to the group. Individuals belong to various groups which can be formal and informal, such as the family, religious groups, leisure groups, professional groups. Each of these groups will influence the behaviour of its members though it is important to remember that people remain as individuals and can make up their own minds. In education there are well-defined formal groups such as courses and classes, and we know that students tend to form strong relationships with others in their groups and therefore modes or norms of behaviour are developed. This socialization process takes place from the moment students begin their courses. They have to learn, for example, not only the subjects taught, but also how to relate to lecturers and fellow students. They learn when it is acceptable to claim the attention of the lecturer and to ask questions, and when conversation with other students is permitted. The teaching methods may require that they cultivate group and presentation skills, and these skills may be taught as part of the course. The user-oriented academic librarian should know where the library fits into this socialization and be prepared to influence it in ways that are considered desirable. A study at Manchester Metropolitan University found, for example, that students in different subject areas embarking on enterprise projects received very different advice on use of the library. Whilst management and business students received detailed written advice, art and design students were given very little information and there was a greater emphasis on original ideas provided by the students, uncluttered by what has already been produced (Hodgson 1993).

Librarians also will have norms of behaviour and in a situation which is new to students these norms will have to be observed and learned. In some cases they will already have encountered librarians and their norms of behaviour in other libraries such as public libraries and school libraries, but they do have to learn about the norms for an academic librarian.

A helpful concept in analysis is 'role' – the cluster of norms determining how a person who occupies a status should behave. All norms and roles are subject to change, but the uncertain role of the academic librarian must make it more difficult for users to know how they can benefit from their services. The Fielden Report highlights the difficulty with its comment about those librarians who normally have most interaction with users: 'On our visits there was a wider range of practice in the role of the subject or information librarian (where it existed) than in any other post' (John Fielden Consultancy 1993, p.26). 'Status' is allocated to individuals in terms of the respect, prestige and influence accorded through ascription and/or achievement. Status is accorded by other people, and the status of academic librarians is therefore given to them by users, administrators, managers, funding bodies and so on. Librarians have had a status problem in many institutions, no more so than in further education. A recent report of a round table meeting highlights the problem and the Library Association offers advice and help to college librarians to give them confidence in their own abilities. 'The results will be better services for our users and an improved status for college librarians' (Clayton 1996, p.20). One of the major failings identified among college librarians was 'lack of recognition that they were part of an organization' (ibid.). Later chapters are designed to show what librarians need to do to involve themselves in the educational enterprise and to avoid damaging isolation.

Norms and roles cause people to act in accordance with the expectations of others. Social roles involve mutual expectations – users expect certain behaviour from librarians and librarians expect certain behaviour from users. Some of this behaviour will be influenced by rules, regulations, user charters and so on, but much of it will result from experience. Users who are badly treated will expect similar treatment again and will tell others about it, whilst it is well known that users have high expectations where services are good and tend to make even greater demands which cannot always be met. Millson-Martula and Menon (1995, pp.33–47), reviewing the research, state that 'in most cases, customers hold expectations that can be considered basic. In general, customers expect a basic solid service and promises that are kept', and the findings of Zeithaml, Parasuraman and Berry (1990) discussed in the previous chapter, are cited in support.

User satisfaction represents the difference between what the users expect and what they get. Whilst objective criteria are frequently used to measure performance, satisfaction is subject to the perceptions of individuals. Millson-Martula and Menon (1995, p.38) believe that 'academic libraries should attempt to exceed the expectations of their customers. This often involves surprising or delighting their customers, doing the unexpected, or providing in a unique way something that their customers consider significant.'

User studies

Academic librarians who apply these analytical tools to their own user communities will be building up a rich picture which should enable them to improve services and predict the consequences of changes more accurately. A great deal of this information will have been gathered from their own participation in activities involving users, ranging from attendance at course committees to answering questions on enquiry desks. These processes are by their nature unsystematic in finding out about user needs but they provide an invaluable context for more systematic investigations. It would be quite wrong, therefore, for a library to undertake investigations and to ignore these understandings, which will have been built up over a number of years. This is not to say that there will be no partial or self-selective understandings which may be hiding the real 'truth' but where, for example, an effective subject librarian has been working successfully with users for many years, any study of his or her community ought to involve him or her in the planning of an investigation and in the interpretation of its findings. Many academic libraries are employing outside consultants to carry out investigations, often with ready-made tools such as questionnaires which can helpfully allow comparisons among different libraries. Priority Search Ltd of Sheffield, for example, have helped a number of colleges in this way. As we have seen, however, with many of the ranking and performance indicator exercises, the context of the findings needs to be made clear and appreciated when comparisons are presented.

The methods of investigation in common use can be looked at as two groups – those which do not directly involve those being investigated and those that do. Prominent in the first group is observation. As Moser (1971, p.244) comments, 'social scientists . . . are literally surrounded by their subject-matter . . . have only to open their eyes to observe their fellow-men and women, and the institutions and societies they have created, in action'. Observation does lend itself to the study of institutions such as universities, where members can quite easily be seen going about their business regularly in a relatively enclosed environment about which there is plenty of documentation. In non-participant observation, or 'bird-watching', observers try to conceal their purpose, watch what is happening, and record the results. If the purpose can be concealed, users will be observed behaving in their normal manner. What is observed will necessarily be selective and affected to some extent by the observer's own experience and perceptions. As part of his study of promotional activities in polytechnic libraries, Atkinson employed non-participant observation. 'This observation was carried out on arrival, so that the perceptions of the researcher were fresh and not influenced by interviews or by a growing personal knowledge of the library' (Atkinson 1992, p.80). It is often difficult to carry out detailed observations satisfactorily such as listening to conversations at enquiry desks or watching users consulting library catalogues. Technology can help in these situations. Microphones could be installed at counters and computer systems are able to record information about catalogue use. Observation as an outsider will not reveal the meanings of the behaviour to the actor except through oral and body language clues. Thus a catalogue user might express frustration more evidently at an interview than in the eyes of an observer. To overcome these problems, social scientists have turned to participant observation, taking the view that 'the understanding of actors' meanings . . . can only be achieved by putting oneself in the actor's place and seeing "reality" as he or she sees it' (Bilton et al. 1987, p.541). Much of the literature on this method is concerned with the problems of truly becoming part of the community being examined, whether the true position of the investigator should be revealed, and the extent to which the investigator should participate in the activities of the actors under study. If we were studying deviancy or life in an unfamiliar community these would be real problems, but virtually all professional librarians in academic libraries have been students and some have been academics. It would not be difficult for a librarian to enrol on a course and to report on perceptions of the library and library use. A helpful development in participatory methodology has been 'cooperative enquiry'. The view is taken that:

If the behaviour of those being researched is directed and determined by the researcher, the research is being done on them and they are not present in the research as persons. One can only do research with persons in the true and fullest sense, if what they do and what they experience as part of research is to some significant degree directed by them. So persons can only properly study persons when they are in active relationship with each other, where the behaviour being researched is self-generated by the researchers in a context of cooperation. (Reason 1995, p.41)

Thus a group of users could undertake a cooperative enquiry with a participant investigator such as a fellow user, student or academic, into information-gathering behaviour.

Loans analysis is carried out by all academic libraries though the amount of sophistication varies greatly, particularly the extent to which the analysis is linked to user categories. Many computerized circulation systems are able to analyse the borrowing of various categories of material by groups of users. The analysis which offers most is that which provides information on borrowings by students on different courses in different years of those courses. Not only is this information useful for stock-building but also politically. For example, if it can be shown that a wide variety of students borrow management material, the case for a library service equally accessible to all members of the community is stronger. The cost centre approach in some institutions has stressed ownership and control of what is paid for, and at its extreme has resulted in departmental libraries available mainly to members of the cost centre. It is important to note that the loan of an item does not necessarily involve use. Quite often an item will be borrowed as a substitute for an item which the user sought, perhaps from a reading list. Librarians are keen that this should happen, for it is well known that lecturers are not necessarily up to date with the literature on their subjects and are likely to appreciate material in coursework which is not copied from familiar sources. It is, however, possible that the borrowed item is quickly discarded and 'document exposure' (eye contact with the material) is minimal. This information can only be obtained by other methods such as interviews and questionnaires.

It is highly probable, on the other hand, that citation analysis is a better indication of use. Hipgrave (1979), for example, studied the use of literature by social scientists through the analysis of references in theses and follow-up articles based on the theses. He came to a number of conclusions about social scientists as a result, such as their dependence on the periodical and the low use of foreign language material. Locally citation analysis has a lot to offer. Although a struggle to obtain consistently, reading lists are routinely used by academic librarians to aid the management of stock. Analysis of references in the work of students may duplicate the reading lists but would more clearly show what has actually been used and found helpful. Similarly citation analysis of the writings of academic staff and researchers should also reveal their uses of the literature.

Methods which require the cooperation of the users have to gain their support if the investigations are to be successful, especially where the user has to invest time in the activity. Nowhere is this better illustrated than in diary keeping. If a number of randomly selected users were to record their uses of the library over a period of time, the value of the information produced would be potentially great. Investigators will usually try to reduce the burden on the respondent by structuring the recording schedule. A diary could be structured chronologically and/or with predetermined headings conforming to the ways in which a person could be expected to use the library, plus a facility for recording anything which did not fit any of the headings provided. Of course any structuring by the investigator does influence the way in which records are kept and inferences drawn, but this has to be weighed against the time-saving advantages to the user and the ease of analysis. Harrop (1981, pp.2–6), for example, used diaries in an investigation of the information needs of undergraduates and asked the following questions: '(a) Were *any* suggestions or recommendations made in your lecture this week about what work you should do, e.g. reading references etc? (b) If so, what were they? (c) If so, how much of the recommended work will you have tried to do by next week's lecture?'

On the face of it, failure surveys appear not to take up too much of a user's time. Typically users are asked to complete slips which indicate what they were looking for and whether they found it. Library staff subsequently check why the item was not found. This is not always because the item is not available, but also for other reasons such as the user's failure to search in the 'correct' manner or the misfiling of the item. The method can therefore tell us as much about the library's failure to provide user-friendly systems and to educate users effectively as about its stock limitations. The information provided by failure surveys is only a starting-point towards an understanding of users' behaviour. It would, for example, be of great benefit to know what efforts the user made to find the item, but this could only be revealed through further written or oral information obtained at the time of the investigation, and would take up more of users' time when they are likely to be in a hurry at the end of their library visit.

In the minds of most people, surveys mean questionnaires, and the design of the questionnaire is frequently considered to be the main task of the investigator. This is a pity because other methods have much to commend them where the circumstances and the objectives of the study are appropriate, and a greater understanding can result from the use of a variety of survey instruments. The questionnaire can either be completed by the respondent unaided or by an interviewer. In the first case questionnaires are commonly sent by post, so the onus is on the respondent to understand the questions and be prepared to spend time answering them. The worries of participant observers about understanding their subjects and the domination of the investigator seem minor compared with similar problems involved in the use of postal questionnaires. Investigators have to try to put themselves in the position of the typical respondent and understand what is needed to obtain full cooperation. To begin with, the investigator has to persuade the respondent that the survey is worthwhile. The letter which accompanies questionnaires needs clearly to emanate from a respectable source, and indicate the purpose of the survey and how the findings will be used, including a note about the confidential nature of the information obtained. A good example is the letter sent with Erens's survey of United Kingdom academics on the importance of academic research and how well university and polytechnic libraries were meeting research needs. Written on British Library Research and Development Department headed notepaper, it states:

In order to obtain an accurate picture of the demands being placed on library services, it is essential to collect information from a representative cross-section of academic staff in universities and polytechnics. Your name has been selected at random from the Commonwealth University Yearbook (in the case of universities) or from staff lists provided by your personnel department (in the case of polytechnics), and I am writing now to ask you to participate in this study. (Erens 1991)

In the same way the status of the enquiry, the reasons for it, and its importance and usefulness have to be communicated quickly by interviewers to potential respondents to obtain their cooperation. In addition, the confidential nature and anonymity of respondents, together with the time it will take, should be made known. This will be made easier if there has been some publicity about the survey, and offence is avoided if permission has been obtained where necessary and where it has been polite to ask. For example, permission should be sought from appropriate subject departments before carrying out a survey of students studying a particular subject.

Most investigative interviewing lies on a continuum between formal questioning, with the wording decided beforehand and with answers restricted, to informal questioning, with a number of topics raised at appropriate times. The latter may ultimately provide more information but is very time-consuming and difficult to analyse. The former will provide restricted information and may be heavily biased towards the interviewer's perception. A technique which helps to avoid this bias is probing, which aims to obtain a response from an informant or a more extensive or explicit expression of it by using neutral questions such as, 'Can you explain a little more fully?'

Bias can also occur because of the way questions are asked and answers interpreted through an interaction of personalities. Age, race, education, religion and gender, for example, can lead to bias, as can perceptions, attitudes, expectations and motives of the interviewer and interviewee. Interviews carried out by library staff or by academic staff known to the students are liable, therefore, to bias. Interviewers have to be aware of these dangers and training is essential. Interviewers also have to think carefully about the location of the interview so that a place will be chosen which will not inhibit the interviewee. Slater (1988, p.229), for example, in her investigation into the information needs of social scientists, found that interviewing at a person's home rather than workplace was preferable: 'Would the local government practitioner who exasperatedly described working in a certain borough in terms of total chaos have been so forthcoming, had she been at her desk, surrounded by her listening staff, whose flagging morale she is desperate to maintain? Somehow I doubt it.'

A useful method of questioning is to focus on 'critical incidents' which isolate important events in a person's experience. Andrews (1991, pp.5–14) employed the technique in exploring students' library use problems with six prompts:

Can you remember a time:
(1)   When you could not find what you were looking for?
(2)   When you found what you wanted easily?
(3)   When you did not know what to do?
(4)   When you were reluctant to ask for help?
(5)   When you received a lot of help?
(6)   When you felt you were treated badly?

A fairly inexpensive and quick method used extensively in marketing and in a number of library surveys is the focus group interview, defined by Widdows, Hensler and Wycott (1991, p.352) as 'a qualitative research technique involving repeated interviews with small groups of eight to twelve people with the intent of identifying the key concerns or wishes of the groups'. Data obtained from focus groups are often difficult to generalize to the wider population, so are often used as a complement to other studies or to obtain insights that can be tested and used in further work. A script is used to facilitate discussions which may be stimulated by group interaction, though some individuals may dominate discussions and influence others in the group. Most focus group interviews are audiotaped or video-taped as writing down group responses can be very difficult.

Some of the methods, such as structured questionnaires with single-word answers, generate information which is easily analysed, but the richer and often more complicated data obtained by other methods, such as loosely structured interviewing, are more difficult. A method of analysis employed in a number of user studies such as Atkinson (1992) is grounded theory. The emphasis in this approach is on the generation of theories and models inductively from the empirical data in order to build up models of behaviour. Ellis (1993, pp.469–86) discusses the method in detail and has used it himself in studies of the information-seeking patterns of researchers in the social sciences, sciences and the humanities. As a result of his analysis he identified the various steps in information seeking which can be especially helpful when thinking about the processes undergone by the users whom librarians are there to support:

1. 'Starting' is the actual identification of a topic and the commencement of the initial search for information.
2. 'Chaining' or 'chasing' refers to the activity of following up on references by using one citation as a link to other citations.
3. 'Selecting' or 'sifting' or 'differentiating' involves the decision about which to filter out as unwanted material.
4. 'Locating' is the actual finding of the information.
5. 'Monitoring' is the process of maintaining current awareness in a particular area of interest by regularly following particular sources.
6. 'Extracting' refers to the process of systematically working through a particular source to locate material of interest. This involves the reading of material to determine which of the material becomes incorporated into the final report.
7. 'Assembly and dissemination' is the actual drawing together of material for publication or some other form of dissemination. (Folster 1995, pp.88–9).

This chapter has attempted to clear up some of the terminological problems associated with the study of users and has introduced concepts and approaches which can contribute towards an understanding of user needs. Those survey methods considered most consistent with these approaches have also been discussed. The way, therefore, has been prepared for a consideration of the various groups of academic library users beginning with the most numerous – the students.

References

Andrews, Judith (1991), 'An exploration of students' library use problems', *Library review,* **40**(1), 5–14.

Atkinson, Peter Jeremy (1992), *Investigation of the effectiveness of promotional activities in Polytechnic libraries*, M.Phil. thesis, Newcastle upon Tyne: Newcastle Polytechnic.

Baker, David (1986), *What about the workers?*, London: Association of Assistant Librarians.

Bilton, Tony, et al. (1987), *Introductory sociology*, 2nd edn, London: Macmillan.

Clayton, Carl (1996), 'Lack of status due to image problem', *Library Association Record*, **98**(1), January.

Cohen, Percy S. (1968), *Modern social theory*, London: Heinemann.

Ellis, David (1993), 'Modeling the information-seeking patterns of academic researchers: a grounded theory approach', *Library Quarterly*, **63**(4).

Erens, Bob (1991), *Research libraries in transition: academic perceptions of recent developments in university and polytechnic libraries*, London: British Library Research and Development Department (Library and Information Research Report 82).

Folster, Mary B. (1995), 'Information seeking patterns: social sciences', *Reference Librarian*, 49/50.

Green, Andrew (1990), 'What do we mean by user needs?', *British Journal of Academic Librarianship*, **5**(2).

Harrop, Cherry (1981), 'The information needs of undergraduates project: some preliminary findings', *CRUS News*, 11, July.

Hipgrave, Richard (1979), *The use of the literature by social scientists*, M.Phil. thesis, Leeds: Leeds Polytechnic.

Hodgson, Marianne (1993), *Information searching for the development of enterprising projects*, Manchester: Manchester Metropolitan University Library.

John Fielden Consultancy (1993), *Supporting expansion: a report on human resource management in academic libraries for the Joint Funding Councils' Libraries Review Group*, Bristol: Higher Education Funding Council for England.

Line, Maurice B. (1974), 'Draft definitions: information and library needs, wants, demands and uses', *Aslib Proceedings*, **26**(2), February.

Line, Maurice B. (1981), 'Ignoring the user: how and why' in *The nationwide provision and use of information*, Aslib–ISS–LA Joint Conference, September 1980, London: Library Association.

Millson-Martula, Christopher and Menon, Vanaja (1995), 'Customer expectations: concepts and reality for academic library services', *College and Research Libraries*, **56**(1), January.

Moser, C. A. (1971), *Survey methods in social investigation*, 2nd edn, London: Heinemann.

Reason, Peter (1995), 'Human inquiry as discipline and practice' in Reason, Peter (ed.), *Participation in human inquiry*, London: Sage.

Slater, Margaret (1988), 'Social scientists' information needs in the 1980s', *Journal of Documentation*, **44**(3), September.

Widdows, Richard, Hensler, Tia A. and Wyncott, Marlaya H. (1991),

'The focus group interview: a method of assessing users' evaluation of library service', *College and Research Libraries*, **52**(1), January.

Zeithaml, Valarie A., Parasuraman, A. and Berry, Leonard L. (1990), *Delivering quality service: balancing customer perceptions and expectations*, London: Collier Macmillan.

4 Students

Because the student population has become so heterogeneous it is difficult to talk about the 'normal' student without falling into clichés. It is possible, however, to refer to trends in student behaviour which do have an effect upon libraries.

Studies and the experiences of librarians all show that students have difficulties using academic libraries. Campbell and Shlechter (1979, pp.26–41) studied student behaviour in the Watson library at the University of Kansas and found that in the interviews 70 per cent of the 'dislike' responses fell into the categories of physical environment and library organization, and in the diaries kept by students there was similar dissatisfaction with the design of the building and the crowding found there. Andrews (1991) also found dissatisfaction in Manchester Polytechnic (now the Metropolitan University) where students invariably reported problems caused by the floor layout. These problems lead to further difficulties when they try to locate material. Although the catalogue might indicate that a book is not on loan, it may not be found on the shelves. As librarians we are well aware of a variety of explanations – misplaced on the shelves, stolen, at binding, on the returns trolley, being read in the library, awaiting repair and so on, but the student is at a loss what to do: 'I came back on four occasions to look for this book and each time the computer said that it was in and it wasn't on the shelf or anywhere near and I didn't know what else to do' (Andrews 1991, p.9). An assumption that the student is looking in the right place may be incorrect since some students do not understand the classification system. The physical separation of subjects which they have studied together, such as social and political history located in the Dewey 300s and 900s, causes annoyance. Understandably most people would like all the material they need to be together in one place and don't always understand the impossibility of achieving this for each person.

To some extent short loan collections fulfil this want and they can be particularly effective in the early part of a course, but information skills needed later are not being developed:

The nature of the subject, the teaching method and assessment mode can help or hinder the development of a more information conscious student, who might be receptive to more in-depth user education once experience has shown the need for more knowledge and expertise ... A high level of directed reading without much encouragement to search for information unaided, combined with the pressures of continuous assessment seems to be the least conducive environment for developing information skills. (Day 1983, p.16)

There is certainly a danger of short loan collections becoming the most used libraries within libraries.

Untidy shelves also cause problems, sometimes exacerbated by the students themselves, who do not replace books in the correct places, particularly in art and design sections where books are often left all over tables and the floor. Whether students are capable or patient enough to replace material in the correct place is questionable, and this is not surprising as most libraries have parallel or separate sequences for different sizes and types of material and, to the uninitiated, it is not clear how mixtures of letters and numbers or decimal points indicate order. Andrews (1991, p.9) also found that students had difficulties with the 'loads of numbers after the decimal point' in some subjects not familiar to Dewey in 1876. A good example of the way in which librarians can fail to realize that what is 'common sense' to them may not be obvious to users is that the books are arranged from top to bottom in fairly narrow bays. I remember staff laughing about a shelver who thought that the books were arranged along the top shelves of all the bays in a row and then along the second shelves and so on. Checks on shelving performed by student shelvers at Manchester Metropolitan University showed great deficiencies in their knowledge of the way materials were arranged, and most of these were students of librarianship!

The solution to many of these problems is effective user education, which starts from an understanding of students' perceptions plus changes that can be made which can make life easier for students. The University of Kansas, for example, concluded from their research findings that 'library planners can assist student users by placing the most central facilities close to the main entrance as well as in close proximity to each other' (Campbell and Shlechter 1979, p.38). Students, like most other people, prefer to take the route of least effort. They will choose to study in quite noisy areas rather than walk up flights of stairs. They will sit close to friends but prefer to have space around them rather than sit next to strangers. Thus libraries are frequently perceived as full when the empty seats are in places where the student does not wish to sit.

Noise

As libraries have become more crowded they have also become noisier. More students are unfamiliar with what has previously been accepted as the norm of library behaviour and prefer to talk in the library when they feel like it and listen to music on their walkmans. Society generally, especially young people, has become more tolerant of noise, but perhaps a little more selfish. Academic libraries have had to cope with the dilemma of providing a welcoming environment but one in which users do not prevent others from working. Campbell and Shlechter (1979) found that 72 per cent of the observed activities were reading and writing but 6 per cent were talking. In some academic libraries noise from talking has become a normal occurrence, sometimes tolerated, but I sense that there has been a movement towards insisting on silence and where possible providing rooms for legitimate group work. It is also in the library's interest to support the provision of places in institutions where students can relax and talk, especially when they are between lectures and are only able to spend short periods in the library. An especially relevant observation was made by Atkinson when he noted a 'trend to greater criticism of environmental conditions being made by people who spent a longer time in the libraries (for example, students and library staff being more critical than academic staff)' (Atkinson 1992, p.25).

Many libraries are now attacking noise by saturating the library with warning notices and threatening punishment for transgressors.

Student confusion

Not only do students have difficulty finding their way round libraries, but also they are not very good at searching for information. A review of the American literature by Kunkel, Weaver and Cook (1996, p.430) provides confirmation and their own investigation led them to the conclusion that:

Lower-level students are confused about the scope and diversity of library resources. They have difficulty interpreting the bibliographical records in the OPAC and in periodical indexes. The terminology of library research is unfamiliar to them. They lack the critical judgement to both select appropriate sources and develop strategies for finding information when their efforts first fail. They also do not have the experience and skills to use information technologies effectively. (Kunkel, Weaver and Cook 1996, p.432)

At the University of Sheffield Wood et al. (1996, pp.79–92) tested undergraduates to establish how they searched databases and discovered that about two-thirds of the searches had serious weaknesses: 'Many students were unable to construct an adequate search query, devise an effective search strategy or achieve an adequate search result.'

As society becomes increasingly 'information-rich', students are able to 'choose from a variety of information sources, such as reference books, multimedia systems, friends, colleagues, films, computer-based training and so forth' (Yacci 1994, p.327) and with student-centred learning placing more emphasis on independence or student-oriented group work, it is becoming essential to provide information-skills teaching programmes. 'For the instruction to be meaningful, it should be actively learned and integrated into the undergraduate curriculum by relating it directly to course subjects. Undergraduates' motivation to learn new skills will be affected by their perceived relevance' (Wood et al. 1996, p.79). There has been a good deal of research into different patterns of learning (cognitive learning patterns) which affect the searching behaviour of individuals. Wood et al. (1996, p.91) conclude that:

It should be worth making students aware of their own cognitive and learning styles and the effect these might have on both learning and searching for information. It should also be worthwhile to design teaching materials which provide intellectual content and approaches which suit different cognitive and learning styles. Because of the facilities available, it may be easier to do this with CAL [computer-assisted learning] packages than with other teaching materials.

Library anxiety

The feelings students have when trying to find information for the first time have been summed up as 'library anxiety' by Mellon (1986, pp.160–5). In her researches she found a large percentage of the students describing their initial response in terms of feeling lost, fearful or anxious. She concluded that:

1. Students' fears are due to a feeling that other students are competent at library use while they alone are incompetent.
2. This lack of competence is somehow shameful and must be hidden.
3. Asking questions reveals their inadequacies. (Mellon 1988, p.138)

Andrews (1990, pp.70–1) found similar responses in her Manchester survey such as:

'I do get very hot and uncomfortable and edgy. It's part of the feeling that makes you not want to try again, you get to the point where you just want to get out. I have spoken to others since we spoke about this, we've chatted about this and a lot of people find the library threatening, they're not happy in it, they want to get out.'

There is also some reluctance to ask library staff for help. Day (1983, p.19) was told by students that staff would feel they ought to know, and examples quoted by Andrews (1990, p.66) appear to confirm this:

A first year Fine Arts student, having great difficulty understanding the Dewey classification scheme, described an incident where a librarian helped him but in such a way that his problem was not solved:
  'But she explained it to me as if I was very silly if I didn't understand it, "it's obvious, the numbers are up there, it's 709 and then . . ." But that didn't help, it didn't answer any questions for me. So it puts you off asking.'

By contrast a Politics student was very pleased with her treatment:

'I needed to look at back issues of newspapers and I went to ask and the librarian came to show me . . . She didn't make me feel stupid and didn't seem to feel that she should be doing some-thing more important with her time, she seemed like that was what she was meant to be doing and she gave me her full time.' (Andrews 1990, p.70)

Both these incidents illustrate how the behaviour of library staff can influence the behaviour of the students.

It may also be thought that students who experience anxiety associated with real or anticipated oral interaction with another person (communication apprehension) would be less likely to ask library staff for assistance. Observational studies by Led-erman (1991, pp.382–9) found that at least it did not influence the initiation of the interaction. Attempting to explain these findings, Lederman makes interesting observations. Perhaps environmental factors nullify the experience of anxiety:

It may be that an institutionalized and thereby familiar procedure for finding information is what reduces his anxiety in that environment, including a routine help (i.e. adopting the norm that the librarian is there to be asked). If this is the case, the more alike libraries are and the more normative the procedures for behavior, including approach behavior, the more likely the environment will be nonthreatening to the library user. (Lederman 1991, pp.386–7).

On the other hand, it is surmised that the very complexity of the library forces the apprehensive person to approach the librarian since 'talking is perceived as less threatening than managing the complex environment on one's own' (Lederman 1991, p.387). Lederman concludes that librarians serve 'a dual function: how to find information and how to communicate competently. In order to do these effectively, they have to be trained to meet the user's communication as well as information needs' (Lederman 1991, p.388).

As expected, students normally find asking friends and col-leagues less stressful than asking library staff: 'I find it very much easier to go and ask a friend, and say "how do you work this?" especially as you're a third year student and you're supposed to know how to use all these things' (Andrews 1991, p.13). Andrews found this happening in three ways: asking for information about the availability of a service, several students working together to solve a library problem, and one student actively teaching another.

Theft and mutilation of stock

Until fairly recently academic librarians did not worry too much about theft and mutilation of stock, though attention has been paid to preservation and emergency planning, but during the last decade or so they have become much more aware of the problem and have had to take action. Concerned predominantly with making material readily available, they have taken some time to 'accept that by securing materials, by making the library a safe place for patrons to come to, they *are* preserving access. After all, while the book or manuscript may be more difficult to get to, at least it's on the shelf in one piece' (Lifer 1994, p.35).

Writing about the Brotherton Library in the University of Leeds, Carr (1991, p.7) points out the contrast between the past and the present:

In 1936 . . . the newly-opened Brotherton Library had fewer than 2,000 readers, most of whom would be known personally to the Library staff, and an 'ethos of trust' generally prevailed. To-day the Library has about 26,000 readers, many of whom come from far afield and are little known; and sad to say, the staff can no longer afford to 'trust' even the regulars. In 1936, the building also had none of the security problems emanating from over-crowding . . . , since it housed fewer than 20,000 volumes in a space which currently holds the best part of a million items.

The survey of theft and loss from UK libraries carried out by Burrows and Cooper (1992) revealed a loss of between 1.9 and 2.1 per cent of the total stock of academic libraries. In large academic libraries the loss will amount to a substantial number of items. The survey also found that there were higher losses of new acquisitions and it is likely that material needed for study such as books and periodical articles on reading lists are most at risk. Academic institutions estimated that 17 per cent of losses were from the non-return of legitimately borrowed items.

Judged by the number of students being caught by security devices, it does appear that theft and attempted theft have increased as the number of students has increased. Unfortunately, the frequency of deliberate mutilation of materials has also grown. Academic libraries (Burrows and Cooper 1992, p.19) believe that the removal of journal articles is the most frequent form of mutilation, followed by writing or drawing on pages.

It is the function of library regulations to control the behaviour of users but it is not always easy to predict their effect. High levels of fines for the late return of items, highly restrictive periods of loan, and strict limits on the number of loans permitted may have the desired effect on some, whilst they may serve as a source of temptation to others to remove the material illegally.

The penalties which might be imposed if regulations are ignored are also meant to affect user behaviour by acting as deterrents. An example of a good statement is quoted by Fox (1991, p.51): 'Any reader removing library material of any kind in contravention of these regulations, or deliberately damaging or mutilating library material, may be liable to a fine, suspension from borrowing or suspension from the library and may be required to pay for the costs of replacement of the material.'

It is important that the library is not seen as operating independently from the rest of the institution in carrying out sanctions. At the very least the institution should be aware of the library's activities and, since the students are primarily members of courses and departments, it is preferable for the academic disciplinary code to be used and for academic staff to decide on the punishments for their own students, with library staff present to give evidence. Librarians sometimes feel that academic staff are too easy on students, do not understand the problems caused by theft and mutilation of material and are perhaps too concerned with worrying about how students will be affected by being banned from the library and the problems this might cause in examination boards, but it is the task of the librarians to make their case.

It can be difficult to prove that students are guilty of theft since legally they not only have to appropriate dishonestly another person's property, but also have to have the intention of permanently depriving the other person of the property. This can present problems, especially with the non-return of borrowed material. Because of this, and because disciplinary hearings can be time-consuming, some libraries impose a caution payment which can be reclaimed in say twelve months' time if the student has not transgressed again.

The ultimate sanction which can be taken by the institution is to refuse to grant students their degrees until all debts are paid and material returned. Cox (1991, p.52) claims that this has worked as a powerful incentive to pay up and return materials.

Amnesties which permit students to return material without paying fines were found by Burrows and Cooper (1992, p.30) to be used by 38 per cent of academic libraries surveyed. Although some were said to have been successful, it does seem doubtful morally to charge some who return material late and not others, and it would be counter-productive to hold them frequently as students could simply wait for the next one rather than return materials.

It is essential that library staff are trained to deal with users who may be attempting to steal material and may be resentful, abusive and aggressive. It is a good idea, for example, to move confrontations away from public areas where possible. 'Where there is an audience both the reader and the librarian will find it more difficult to adopt a reasonable posture and the resolution of the problem will take significantly longer or may not even be possible to achieve' (Lancaster 1991, p.56). Moving confrontations away from counters and library exits should also allow professional staff to come to the aid of library assistants and security staff. My own experience also leads me to agree strongly with Cox (1991, p.53) that 'there is little more demoralizing for security personnel than to face confrontations with readers who are misbehaving and then to discover repeatedly that the matter goes no further'.

Increased access

In the 1990s higher education has been undergoing a 'revolution as profound as that in the mid-1960s . . . a transition from an elite to a mass system' with access moving 'from the margins to the centre of higher education policy debate' (Smith, Scott and Mackay 1993, p.316–7). Lieven (1989, pp.160–74) has identified four ideological positions which have been taken to justify increased access. The first, serving the need of the individual for self-fulfilment, has always been at the heart of the liberal tradition of education – a tradition strongly supported by many librarians from the founders of the public library movement to the present day. Closely related to this tradition is the radical commitment to empowering the traditionally disadvantaged and disenfranchised. Again many librarians are familiar and sympathetic to this approach as they try to help those who have not had the same opportunities as others. This was particularly the case for public librarians during the 1970s (Jordan 1975, pp.62–6). The equal opportunities movements, together with evidence from reviews of the public library services in the 1990s, have seen a revival of interest (Pateman 1996, pp.362–3), whilst it has always been a concern in areas of deprivation as librarians seek to meet the needs of those who are not traditional library users. In further and higher education there has not been the same 'revolutionary' commitment, but there is a desire to support those who have gained admission but are unfamiliar with libraries and systematic information seeking. Both the Dearing (National Committee of Inquiry into Higher Education 1997) and the Kennedy (Kennedy 1997) Reports, however, have focused upon the need for widening participation in higher and further education respectively. The Kennedy Report goes as far as to propose that the Further Education Funding Council should divert more of its resources to poorly qualified people by awarding cash 'in inverse proportion to students' previous level of achievement' and the poor should be helped by taking into account 'relative levels of social deprivation using post codes' (p.56).

These altruistic motives contrast with the far more self-interested third position, which Lieven calls the 'institutional imperative' – institutions need to admit more students to keep up their numbers as the traditional school leaver intake reduces due to demographic changes and institutions have to compete with each other in a more hostile financial and market environment. Lieven's final position is vocational commitment – training a workforce for the economy and therefore concentrating on the expansion of those areas favoured by the government and industry. Smith, Scott and Mackay's analysis of mission statements and strategic plans showed that the older universities were continuing 'to espouse the traditional liberal cause of serving the individual's need for self-fulfilment' and students from disadvantaged backgrounds 'will be expected to conform to expectations of high entry standards' (Smith, Scott and Mackay 1993, p.332). On the whole such students are treated like any other students and are expected to sort things out for themselves. This approach has been the one most likely to be pursued by librarians in older universities. In the new universities 'there is much evidence of a desire to empower the disadvantaged and, in a significant number of cases, this is approached in a fashion which expects radical change to accrue from their policies' (Smith, Scott and Mackay 1993, p.332) . The larger numbers of non-traditional students admitted to the new universities in the past has probably been a factor in the greater support given in the form, for example, of user education. Both older and new universities are very much concerned with institutional survival and, if this means becoming more hospitable to non-traditional groups, institutions of all types will adopt such policies and librarians will be expected to adapt to meet their needs.

Smith, Scott and Mackay's taxonomy of access strategies adopted by institutions provides a useful overview prior to more detailed discussion of the user groups most involved (Smith, Scott and Mackay 1993, pp.323–4):

- an expansion of student numbers, including European Community and overseas students;

- an expansion of course provision, including pre-degree, undergraduate and postgraduate/post experience courses;
- a widening of access, with particular reference to the following kinds of students;
  - (a) mature
  - (b) part-time
  - (c) those with non-traditional qualifications
  - (d) students from non-traditional or disadvantaged backgrounds defined in socio-economic terms, ethnicity or gender;
- students recruited from the immediate locality and/or region;
- affording access to students on the basis of credit accumulation and transfer;
- making exit/entry and choice more flexible by modularisation of course structure;
- encouraging access by franchise agreements by which other institutions deliver courses on behalf of the higher education institution.

Since these strategies are published by institutions and in many cases are vigorously pursued, it is in the library's interest to play its part.

Overseas students

The development of the European Community has led to greater liaison amongst its members. Many more European students are spending some time in the United Kingdom, often as a result of exchange schemes. There have always been considerable numbers of foreign students, especially in higher education institutions, with historical links with Commonwealth countries providing a distinct encouragement, and many institutions are marketing their courses abroad hoping to benefit from the higher fees paid by students from overseas. In the United States it has been estimated that there are more than one million foreign students studying in American universities (Liu 1995, pp.239–46).

The problems overseas students encounter do, of course, vary with the country of origin and their previous experiences. Most will have some difficulty adjusting to cultural differences, some of which are reflected in the library's practices. Baker's survey at the Liverpool School of Tropical Medicine (Baker 1990, pp.509–10) showed that 46 per cent of overseas students on four courses had had little or no experience of using libraries. Wise (1988, pp.1–2) refers to previous experiences of restricted access to library materials and the difficulty of adjusting to open access and Dennison (1991, pp.16–17) stresses the need not only to inform overseas students of the library rules and regulations but to explain the reasons for them, so that they will understand how they are expected to behave, what is not acceptable and what will happen if they transgress. Some will have had no experience of information technology – 'one student thought that there were actually more computers in Heriot-Watt University than in his own country' – but librarians must 'beware of assuming that such is always the case. Information technology is spreading very rapidly in some developing countries' (McLeod 1993, pp.18–19). Some will also encounter language problems. Although English is the nearest to a universal language, they are unlikely to have encountered English spoken quickly and in a variety of accents. Library staff need to be aware of this problem, which can be exacerbated by the use of library jargon unfamiliar to overseas users. Liu recommends a four-step approach with the first step establishing an

open conversational decorum that facilitates the talk about the problems . . . The second step is to learn to differentiate goal-oriented talk from metatalk, especially to learn to engage in metatalk . . . 'talk about talk' during which the librarian rephrases the question and makes sure the actual purpose of the question is identified. The third step is to make explanations relative rather than absolute . . . For example, many foreign students may not understand what 'stack' means . . . if the librarian explains that stacks are bookshelves, and distinguishes 'reference stacks' from 'periodical stacks' confusion can be eliminated. Finally all explanations about the problem should be made relevant to foreign students' lifeworld. For example, if you refer a student to the open stacks, you may ask if they have open stacks or self-service stacks in their own country. (Liu 1995, pp.242–3)

It is not unusual for foreign students to arrive late, after term has begun, and some may come for a period in the middle of an academic year. They will therefore have missed the induction received by other students, including library induction.

There is a view that there is no need to make special provision for overseas students and in hard-pressed libraries this is an understandable position to adopt, but it does mean that overseas students will initially be at a disadvantage and, where their stay is short, it may never be repaired. Accounts of measures taken suggest that most of the problems can be alleviated by targeted seminars provided in addition to normal induction sessions and later on, so as to include late-comers. McLeod (1993, pp.18–19) has described successful sessions organized by Heriot-Watt University Library which are informal and include refreshments. Various library leaflets are discussed and the students are asked to think of any two questions they may have about the library. These are answered in the final stages of the seminar, which lasts about one hour. These seminars will work best where personal invitations are sent to new overseas students. To obtain lists it will be necessary to liaise with departments, and in many larger institutions with individuals given special responsibilities for overseas students and with committees set up to encourage the recruitment of overseas students and monitor their progress in the institution. As in most areas of operation, the library should not be working in isolation.

Special leaflets are also seen to be important and can be written in the major languages. They can give advice on where to go for help, how to obtain information about the area such as maps, travel information and telephone directories. A list of books on living in Britain such as those produced by UKCOSA and the British Council might be included, plus a glossary of library terms. There is some demand for material in their own languages particularly newspapers. In cases where the language is taught in the institution there will already be material, but in other cases it is often felt to be too costly and the intention anyway is for overseas students' knowledge of English to improve.

Both Dennison (1991, p.17) and McLeod (1993, p.18) recommend displays. The one at Heriot-Watt is quite an elaborate welcoming display with drawings of people in various national dress superimposed on a sketch of the university campus.

The social action approach (see Chapter 3) can greatly help library staff to appreciate the perceptions of overseas students, enhanced by training seminars addressed by overseas students who are able to explain how they have felt about using the library.

Mature students

In the United States it is reckoned that in the next ten years the 'majority of students will not be the eighteen- to twenty-four-year-olds who come to higher education directly from high schools. Instead, the largest group will be students who are older and attend school on part-time rather than full-time basis'. Hammond (1994, pp.323–41) has summed up the characteristics of mature students and, although she is basing her conclusions on American studies, her findings are complementary to those of United Kingdom studies such as Tunstill (1991): 'These students are pressured because the demands of the home, work and school are often in conflict. Job and employment responsibilities, child care arrangements and transportation considerations are problems for this group of students' (Hammond 1994, p.324).

A quotation from a New Zealand study (Cocklin 1990, pp.195–210), quoted by Tunstill, illustrates just how bad it can get:

I am so tired. I have spent the weekend battling with my 16yr old daughter over her not being allowed out with a friend I do not approve of on Sat. night. Having spent all day mowing the lawns etc. Tonight went to do my typing homework but found the back space on my typewriter does not work. Also not working are my kettle, toaster, clock, iron and my lawn mower is just going and I cannot afford to get them fixed.

The consequence is that mature students do welcome services which help them to save time, and they are likely to be more articulate in their criticisms of inefficient services.

It has been shown that these students are anxious about the new technology, the desire to succeed, and competition from younger students. Additionally a proportion will have difficulty relating to former family and friends as expectations and attitudes begin to change and new friends are made (O'Donohue, H'Orle and Aldridge 1992, pp.40–3). They do therefore require tactful encouragement and support and to be made welcome in an environment which is often more alien to them than to traditional students. With increased student numbers, teaching staff are not always readily available. 'This, combined with the fact that students sometimes found it difficult to approach their personal tutors, means students turn to support staff for help and information. Library staff are among the most accessible of support staff' (O'Donohue, H'Orle and Aldridge 1992, p.41).

Whilst young adults and men are 'most likely to give employment-related reasons for learning, women and older people are more likely to claim that they are learning for personal satisfaction, self development or as an activity' (Blaxter and Tight 1993, pp.13–21). A survey of part-time adult students studying for arts and social studies awards showed that career advancement was low on the list of study purposes, whereas personal development and subject interest were high. The strong personal motivation of many mature students is a strength which can be used by librarians when delivering services and dealing with their problems. Over the last decade or so a lot more attention has been paid to the way adults learn and how this differs from traditional views about children's education – andragogy rather than pedagogy (Knowles 1990).

In a review of changes which have resulted from the application of these theories Sheridan (1986 pp.156–67) is convinced that 'librarians should begin to review their methods and styles in bibliographical instruction classes, at the reference desk, when developing in-house guides, and in our outreach, with this new adult clientele in mind'.

Part-time students

While the number of non-standard students on full-time courses has grown, around two-thirds of mature students are part-time; thus many of the points already made apply to part-timers. Since it is difficult to disentangle the two and assign cause to one characteristic or the other, the practical solutions which might be applied are discussed for both categories.

Those who are part-time spend a smaller proportion of their time on the university or college premises and, when there, they are mostly involved with lectures or tutorials. 'Any spare time is spent grabbing a meal, doing a spot of frantic photocopying or (most important) talking over study matters with fellow students. They tend to find that they are unable to spend enough time on vital study facilities like the university library' (Heery 1993, p.21). Although lack of time is certainly an important factor, McDowell argues that it

is not a sufficient explanation for low levels of library use by part-time students. If it is essential for their course students will find time to use libraries, but there was some evidence that lecturers are conscious of time constraints, and limit the information use of part-time students by the teaching and assessment methods they use. (McDowell 1985, p.7)

It has frequently been stated that the services of most academic institutions and their libraries have remained stubbornly oriented towards the traditional full-time student and have not adapted to serve an increasingly diverse student population. There is evidence of change, though the statement is true for many libraries as shown by Fisher and Moses's survey of UK university libraries in 1990–91 (Fisher and Moses 1991, pp.149–62). It is not necessarily because the needs of part-time students are not understood, but often because positive discrimination towards them affects services to other groups when resources as a whole are in decline, especially where policies of self-help appear to be contradicted. Much of the literature describes special projects and research for which extra funds have been made available, with success more likely where library needs have been examined in the context of the wider needs of mature and part-time students. Administratively it has been easier for libraries to apply solutions to part-time students than to mature students since they are easily identifiable and their status is readily apparent on databases and student identity cards.

Strategies aimed at saving time have naturally been in the forefront among libraries that have addressed the needs of part-time and mature students, particularly special services which are only offered to part-time students. One of the most comprehensive services is that provided by the University of the West of England, where a new additional post of Adviser to Part-time Students was appointed:

She operates a 'phone enquiry service for them that often saves them a visit to the library. She renews books if students ring in ... She reserves items for them and places inter-library loans in response to telephone requests. She will photocopy periodical articles so they are waiting for the student arriving for lectures. Students often send in lists of references and Sue will take whatever action is appropriate to ensure that they obtain the books or articles. Students can request to have up to three books taken from the shelves and kept for them at the issue desk. Sue will advise students over the phone about materials present in the library on subjects they are investigating. She will fax or post articles to students ... She will book sessions for them on the library's CD-ROM machines. (Heery 1993, p.22)

The provision of a special collection of materials available only to part-time students would seem a good idea, but experience has shown them to be little used (James 1991, pp.9–12). A telephone renewals service, however, is popular, especially where fines are high. At Manchester Metropolitan University it became so popular with all users that it had to be restricted to part-time students to enable the library to cope. Many academic libraries have one-week loan facilities for material in demand. The thinking behind this is that part-time students normally attend the institution once a week and short loan collections are of little use. Reservations can be made, though there is no guarantee that material will be returned promptly.

Although some of these services may appear to militate against students learning how to use the library themselves, there are also activities which are designed to inform and encourage self-help. Many libraries produce booklets or leaflets describing services to part-time students such as that issued by Manchester Metropolitan University, and induction programmes are specially designed to guide part-time students. User education programmes have taken account of anxiety over information technology, both with the provision of general sessions and tutorials such as those at Arizona State University West, where 'one-hour sessions on using electronic sources are offered at a wide range of different times, including evenings, weekends, and usual meal times, to accommodate students who are on campus at less conventional hours' (Hammond 1994, p.325).

Part-time students frequently ask for longer opening hours including weekends and evenings, and academic libraries in the UK are increasing their opening hours, with Bath University claiming in 1996 to be the first British university library to open all night ('Bath opens all nighter' 1996, p.605). Experience, however, has shown that longer opening hours suit full-time students more than part-time, probably because of family and domestic commitments. The understandable preference is for services to be available at the times the students attend the institution, but they are in classes for most of that time. Use of the library depends for most students upon the importance given to it by tutors and the rewards available to the student.

Some tutors, aware of the need to consult sources, provide such help themselves through, for example, the distribution of photocopies, notes which summarize material sufficiently for answering examination questions (often set by themselves) or the provision of a box of books. A more satisfactory situation would seem to be for tutors to allow a short period during classes for students to use the library. This, however, depends on convenience of location and on student preferences. Asked whether they would prefer such an arrangement or forego a break and finish early, most classes, in my experience, opt for an early finish and make for the early bus rather than the library. The situation cries out for better liaison between library staff and tutors – exactly Fisher's conclusion following a survey at Bristol University which recommended 'a formal system of liaison between academic and library staff and . . . the establishment of standard procedures in the setting up of new courses' (Fisher and Moses 1991, p.157). In addition Coulter and James (1988, pp.2–5) proclaim that it is not sufficient to have the goodwill and commitment of teaching staff and librarians and liaison between them, but 'considerably more detail in forward planning of student access to learning material is necessary if students are not to be disadvantaged. All those involved in this planning – lecturers as well as course leaders; librarians as well as teaching staff – must see themselves as committed by its outcome' (p.4).

Distance learning

In larger countries with more dispersed populations, such as the USA, Canada and Australia, distance or off-campus students are more prevalent and more attention has been given to library services exemplified by a special issue of *Library Trends* (1991) and the ACRL (Association of College and Research Libraries) guidelines for extended campus library services ('ACRL guidelines' 1990, pp.353–5). In the UK the Open University has been the dominant provider of distance learning education since 1969 and, starting from scratch, has been able to view the needs of its students as its courses have developed. Students receive packages of course material which provide basic information and draw upon other sources. In the first years of study it is expected that the information contained in the course units, together with the recommended texts, many of which are produced especially for Open University students, will be sufficient. The need to search for recommended items is alleviated by the use of 'readers' containing material from a wide range of sources. At more advanced levels systematic use of the literature becomes more important and the university provides guidance on the use of libraries. Public libraries are naturally available and the Open University has made arrangements for access to many academic libraries, though public libraries have expressed concern about students generally as they 'increasingly spill out of their own hard-pressed libraries and overload others' ('Lack of facilities . . .' 1996, p.19). Library access, therefore, is a major problem (Unwin 1994, p.11–20) as public libraries continue to be underfunded, travel to the nearest institution of higher education may be difficult, and access to services such as online searching and inter-library loans may not be available or may be costly. Unwin's survey (Unwin 1994, p.17) found that students were being charged anything from £80 to £20 per year for services at either public or higher education libraries, with some charging extra for inter-library loans and others restricting use to reference only. Some libraries have corporate membership schemes costing between £250 and £400 per year and distance students employed by organizations taking out corporate membership are given the same borrowing rights as registered students. Distance learning through the Open University is backed up by a series of tutorials held in urban centres and by summer schools, and increasing use is made of information technology both in assessment and in coursework:

The Open University is investing £610M over five years developing new approaches to teaching and learning through its new Knowledge Media Institute set up in 1995. New materials are being created to replace paper and talk. Students of art history, for instance, can view a painting on their PC screens and change its composition . . . the Open College has launched a new range of Internet and Intranet services to combat the feeling of isolation suffered by distance learners. (Nicholls 1997, p.ii)

The use of new technology is an area which must develop in the future, but there is a long way to go, even in the USA, where

the extremely low use of home computers for research by all students, and especially by those who are considered nontraditional, indicates a strong need for marketing and training to help students take better advantage of emerging technologies to solve some library-use and time-management problems. It may also be true that fewer students have access to home computers than we assume. If that is the case, the solution may require an institutional response to assist students in acquiring equipment. (Hammond 1994, p.328)

The Open University has been so professional and innovative that it has been difficult for traditional institutions to follow its lead. Where courses have been provided, Fisher's survey of 1989 showed the library support to have been generally poor and 'in terms of the scale of operations, the off-campus work of polytechnics, colleges and some conventional universities fades into insignificance when compared with the work of the Open University' (Fisher 1991, pp.479–94). The type of library service which would suit distance learners is reflected in the areas discussed by Slade (1991, pp.454–78) in his Canadian survey: core collections of materials in accessible locations, a postal request service, a reference answering service including subject searching, telephone access at no cost to the student, user education, and inter-library loans. Perhaps the cost in time and labour of providing first-class distance learning on a level with the Open University and providing library services such as those just listed has led higher education in the UK to pursue franchising and other collaborative arrangements as a way of reaching more students by putting part of the responsibility on the franchisees.

Franchising

A few higher education institutions were involved in franchising activities in the 1980s but the franchising boom did not begin until the early 1990s. The term is now used to describe 'the delivery of the whole or parts of a course in an institution other than the centre in which it is developed and validated' (Woodrow 1993, pp.207–10). Students are usually enrolled as members of the franchisor institution and arrangements are made for the sharing of income with the franchisee in a 'Memorandum of Cooperation' which will include access to resources such as library services. Morris (1993, pp.57–67) has listed the benefits of franchising to the franchisor as:

- a new source of capital
- sharing of risk
- speed of expansion
- the ability to tap new and marginal markets
- exploitation of local knowledge of the franchisee
- 'ownership' of the business by the franchisee

and benefits to the franchisee as:

- less risk
- access to intellectual property of the franchisor
- access to special facilities of the franchisor (e.g. library, computing)
- quality assurance
- sharing in the franchisor's reputation/name
- some degree of local monopoly
- access to funds

The staff and students directly involved in the courses need adequate support from the library, and although provision in further education colleges will not be identical to that of universities, it should be broadly comparable. In most cases the franchised courses will be first years of degrees, diploma courses and pre-degree foundation courses. Progression to the next part of courses, held at the franchisor's institution, is usually automatic on successful completion of the franchised element, though students may choose to continue with another institution on advanced entry arrangements or through the credit accumulation and transfer scheme.

For provision to be adequate there should be involvement by librarians of both institutions prior and during the validation stage so that weaknesses can be discovered and a coordinated effort can be made to improve the situation before the course begins. The Library Association has listed the criteria for library support of franchised courses (Library Association 1992, pp.458 and 460), stating that quality depends on the relationship between library provision and the academic processes of the institution, the involvement of library staff in the college's decision-making arrangements, the adequacy of library resources, including staffing and staff development, and the availability of library services. The main controversy has often been about the availability of the resources and services of the franchisor's library to franchised students. Since many libraries in the further education sector are under-resourced, librarians from franchisor libraries view the improvement of those libraries, on which students are highly dependent, as the priority. Any suggestion that this is less important because they have access to the franchisor's library should be strongly opposed. The franchisor can expect to provide specialist material to support more advanced assignments, and academic staff teaching the courses should be given access to the wider range of resources to prepare their teaching materials. Many franchised courses are located some distance from the franchisor institution, sometimes abroad, so that dependence is even greater on the franchisee's library. In the UK the Higher Education Quality Council's Quality Assurance Group carries out audits on collaborative provision which includes not only franchising but other collaborative arrangements, such as accreditation of courses run by other institutions, and courses run jointly with other institutions. The concern in all these arrangements is that the students have access to the library services which they need to be successful and that the institutions recognize this in the provision of resources.

Students with special needs

Clarke (1995, pp.10–18) has estimated that at least 3 per cent of the student population in higher education may be expected to have some form of disability. 'The percentage of disability rises with age. Almost 70% of disabled adults are 60 or over' (Fleming 1992). With institutions attracting more mature students, providing for people with disability becomes a greater necessity and in the UK the Disability Discrimination Act 1995 'gives new rights to the UK's 6 million disabled people (around 1 in 10 of the population) and will make it unlawful to discriminate against disabled people in the provision of jobs, goods, facilities and services' ('Attitude can be the key' 1996, p.237). Institutions funded by the Further and Higher Education Funding Councils will have to publish information about facilities for disabled students. *The charter for higher education*, published by the Department for Education in 1993, makes frequent mention of facilities for the disabled and states that 'universities and colleges should explain their policies for providing access to students with disabilities or learning difficulties' (Great Britain. Department for Education 1993). The Further Education Funding Councils are likely to implement recommendations of the Tomlinson Committee on Learning Difficulties and/or Disabilities, including the adoption of the concept of inclusive learning – the creation of learning environments to match the specific learning needs and styles of students with learning difficulties/disabilities (Shepherd 1997, p.240). Advice is available from SKILL (The National Bureau for Students with Disabilities). As institutions produce charters and make statements in their prospectuses about services to the disabled, they are likely to attract more of these students.

Some solutions to the problems of the disabled, such as equipment and lifts, are expensive, so that it is easy to understand one comment from Jahoda and Faustino's survey: 'the handicapped are less than 2% of our student body! With the economic situation the way it is, we need funds and positions to serve the other 98% . . . I feel the emphasis on "handicapped" will be short lived as we just can't afford it' (Jahoda and Faustini 1985, p.209). Less expensive are changes in attitudes so that 'all library staff, whatever their level of seniority, must contribute to provide special needs students with a welcoming atmosphere in which they can feel comfortable' (Bell 1994, pp.97–103). Similar positive sentiments are normally included in institutional policy statements on equal opportunities.

Clarke's survey in 1993 (Clarke 1995, pp.13–18) found that far more academic institutions acted reactively rather than pro-actively, in that they responded to needs when asked for help but were less likely actively to identify students or have a service coordinator. There is some difficulty with identification because many disabled students prefer not to be dealt with in a special way as this emphasizes their disability. Some students do not officially admit their disability to the institution and therefore do not appear on registered lists. It is important, however, for the library to have access to lists so that the needs of known disabled students can be met.

Clarke's checklist (Clarke 1995, p.12) of the main barriers to access helps in understanding the problems disabled students face. Those who lack mobility are disadvantaged by a lack of parking space near buildings, by steps, heavy doors, absence of handrails, high counters, narrow spaces between shelves, narrow entrances and corridors, and a lack of specialized toilet space. Fairly straightforward adjustments, some expensive, can be made to alleviate many of these barriers, and good guiding using standard disability symbols is a great help. In the USA a most helpful guide has been produced by Velleman (1990) which includes a chapter on barrier-free design for libraries. Altruism and understanding of other users is also necessary, especially by not obtruding on special car parking spaces.

Those with physical health and stamina difficulties can find books heavy and difficult to take off the shelves and problems may be encountered using equipment. Personal service is offered at the University of the West of England, where the 'Special Service Librarian meets a number of disabled students before the start of their course to discuss their particular needs, how the library is able to respond and to offer individual library tours' (Tooby 1995, pp.46–8). Books can be reserved and renewed by telephone and material can be photocopied for them. Jahoda and Faustini (1985, p.208) have listed the tasks of a library coordinator for the physically disabled and have used it to survey libraries in the South-East of the USA:

1. Determine information needs of physically disabled students and faculty.
2. Instruct physically disabled students in the use of the library.
3. Orient public service library staff on special needs of and resources for physically disabled students and faculty.
4. Coordinate work of library staff as it relates to physically disabled students and faculty.
5. Coordinate work of volunteers as it relates to library service to disabled students and faculty.
6. Provide liaison with organizations serving physically disabled persons.
7. Assist in obtaining outside funding for library service to physically disabled persons.
8. Keep up with developments in information resources and services to physically disabled persons.
9. Conduct a facilities evaluation to identify architectural barriers.
10. Assist in the evaluation of library service to physically disabled students and faculty.

It can be seen that training is an important part of a coordinator's work, and it is accorded prominence in most accounts of services. Graubart (1996, pp.37–40) describes the staff sensitivity training programme at the University of Missouri–Kansas City library. Besides increasing sensitivity and awareness, the aim is to create an image that the library is a helpful place, sensitive to differences in ability. As in other areas the importance of involving the users themselves has to be stressed. In this context it is important to involve a number of different disabled people in the training programme. This is because people with a disability are in the best position to tell you what it is like to be disabled. This said, each person is different and will encounter different problems and adopt different solutions to these problems.

Training should also include the use and maintenance of special equipment. Most of this is designed to help those with impaired vision. Clarke's survey (Clarke 1995, p.15) found that the most popular items were CCTV – a camera which magnifies printed matter on to a monitor – a Kurzweil or similar machine which scans print and outputs via a voice synthesizer, and PCs which scan print, and have voice and Braille output. In the UK the Royal National Institute for the Blind's 'Partnership in Access Scheme', in which the RNIB and the educational institution share the cost, has been used to purchase equipment. The advice frequently given is that low-tech solutions are often more effective and create less difficulty for those with impaired vision. The Centre for Research in Library and Information Management at the University of Central Lancashire, however, is aiming to develop electronic library services for users who are blind or visually impaired in its Reviel project (Livesey and Fisher, 1997 pp.83–4). Large-print material is helpful for those with slighter impairments, though the availability of non-fiction material is limited. Text-enlargement software is also being used to enable students to access library catalogues and networked CD-ROMs. Audiotapes are used by many blind students and there are often reader schemes in which fellow students, library staff and other volunteers tape material. In its survey of higher education institutions in the UK, the Reviel project found that 66 per cent of respondents indicated that they provided a CCTV enlargement facility, 52 per cent magnifiers, 45 per cent scanners with voice output, 44 per cent a Braille production service, 34 per cent production of enlarged print, 20 per cent audio recording of text and 8 per cent tactile diagrams (Livesey and Fisher 1997, p.84).

Bernard Quinn of the British Deaf Association has warned librarians not to put technology before people because it can get in the way of communication (Beal 1996, p.1–2). Communicating face to face is better than hiding behind equipment. When a person has little or no experience of communicating with deaf people it is only natural to feel uncomfortable. Goldmann and Mallory (1992, pp.21–30) advise on the do's and dont's: don't shout as a profoundly deaf person will hear nothing and a hearing aid wearer may experience both distortion and pain; don't lean forward or speak into a deaf person's ear as lipreading is made more difficult, and again, discomfort will be caused to the hearing aid wearer. Do use facial expressions appropriate to the desired meaning and tone of the message. Do keep sentences short, emphasizing key words, and try to avoid sudden changes in the direction of a conversation as they make speechreading more difficult. Speechreading encompasses lipreading but also incorporates other visual clues such as facial expression, gestures, pantomime, rate of delivery and eye contact.

British Sign Language is used by about 50,000 people in the UK and there is a growing interest in learning it. Writing is one of the best ways of getting a message across to a deaf person, and those who have acquired deafness will be able to read in the normal way. Those born profoundly deaf may only be able to read sign language. Videos with sub-titles are particularly useful for deaf people, and various organizations have produced signed videos. The need for a positive attitude towards any user group cannot be overemphasized and 'the desire to communicate and the willingness to adapt as well as possible to the communication needs of the individual deaf person are more important than extensive sign language training' (Goldmann and Mallory 1992, p.29).

This chapter has highlighted the problems students experience when using academic libraries, as well as some of the unacceptable behaviour which is now experienced. As the student body has become increasingly heterogeneous, it has become important for the different needs of the various groups to be properly understood. To meet these needs adequately the problems of each group have to be appreciated, without unhelpful stereotyping of individuals. Liaison with the institution is essential, especially with staff who have special responsibilities for service to groups. It is often desirable for members of the library staff to have special responsibilities for particular groups. Training staff to understand the needs of groups and how these needs might be met is important and such training can be greatly enhanced by the involvement of members of the student groups. Strong relationships with academic staff and early planning of services with them will greatly improve quality. Targeted seminars, leaflets and displays all help to communicate the genuine interest the library has in meeting the needs of student groups.

References

'ACRL guidelines for extended campus library services' (1990), *College and Research Libraries News*, **51**(4), April.

Andrews, Judith (1990), *Manchester Polytechnic Library: a study to investigate the effect and control of change in its internal and external environments*, M.A. thesis, Manchester: Manchester Polytechnic Department of Library and Information Studies.

Andrews, Judith (1991), 'An exploration of students' library use problems', *Library Review*, **40**(1).

Atkinson, Peter Jeremy (1992), *Investigation of the effectiveness of promotional activities in Polytechnic libraries*, M.Phil. thesis, Newcastle upon Tyne: Newcastle Polytechnic.

'Attitude can be the key' (1996), *Library Association Record*, **98**(5), May.

Baker, Susan (1990), 'Providing library services to overseas students', *Library Association Record*, **92**(7), July.

'Bath opens all-nighter' (1996), *Library Association Record*, 98(12), December.

Beal, Anthony (1996), 'Deaf awareness', *NW News* 67, June.

Bell, Suzette (1994), 'Students with special educational needs: how the library can help', in *Online Information 94: 18th international online information meeting proceedings London 6–8 December 1994*, Oxford: Learned Information.

Blaxter, Loraine and Tight, Malcolm (1993), 'I'm only doing it to get in the black gown: dream and reality for adults in part-time higher education', *Journal of Further and Higher Education*, **17**(1), Spring.

Burrows, John and Cooper, Diane (1992), *Theft and loss from UK libraries: a national survey*, London: Home Office Police Department.

Campbell, David E. and Shlechter, Theodore M. (1979), 'Library design influences on user behavior and satisfaction', *Library Quarterly*, **49**(1).

Carr, Reg (1991), 'Problems of security in older library buildings' in Quinsee, A. G. and McDonald, A. C. (eds), *Security in academic and research libraries*, Newcastle upon Tyne: University Library.

Clarke, Hazel (1995), 'Academic library services for students with disabilities (Research project for the Daphne Clark Award 1991/2)', *Library and Information Research News*, 62, Spring.

Cocklin, Barry (1990), 'The adult student at secondary school: a New Zealand case study', *Studies in the Education of Adults*, **22**(2), October.

Coulter, Diana and James, Robert (1988), 'A formative evaluation of provision for part-time students: a case study', *CRUS News*, 32, November.

Cox, Peter (1991), 'Legal processes' in Quinsee, A. G. and McDonald, A. C. (eds), *Security in academic and research libraries*, Newcastle upon Tyne: University Library.

Day, Joan M. (1983), 'Student information use and course demands', *Education Libraries Bulletin*, 26(2), Summer.

Dennison, Pauline(1991), 'Overseas students in an academic library', *U C and R Newsletter*, 35, Winter.

Fisher, Raymond K. (1991), 'Off-campus library services in Higher Education in the United Kingdom', *Library Trends*, **39**(4), Spring.

Fisher, Raymond K. and Moses, Tessa A. (1991), 'Library provision for continuing education students in Britain's universities: a changing scene?', *British Journal of Academic Librarianship*, **6**(1), 1991.

Fleming, Bernard (ed.) (1992), *The accessible librarian information pack*, London: Disability Interest Librarians Group.

Fox, Peter (1991), 'Legal processes' in Quinsee, A. G. and McDonald, A. C. (eds), *Security in academic and research libraries*, Newcastle upon Tyne: University Library.

Goldmann, Warren R. and Mallory, James R. (1992), 'Overcoming communication barriers: communicating with deaf people', *Library Trends*, **41**(1), Summer.

Graubart, Marilyn (1996), 'Serving the needs of students with physical disabilities', *Library Hi Tech*, **53**(14:1).

Great Britain. Department for Education (1993), *The charter for higher education*, London: Department for Education.

Hammond, Carol (1994), 'Nontraditional students and the library:

opinions, preferences, and behaviors', *College and Research Libraries*, 55, July.

Heery, Mike (1993), 'Improving services to part-time students in a university library', *Learning Resources Journal*, **9**(1).

Jahoda, Gerald and Faustini, Paula (1985), 'Academic library service to physically disabled students and faculty', *The Reference Librarian*, 12, Summer/Spring.

James, Rob (1991), 'Library services to part-time students', *Library and Information Research News*, **14**(50), Spring.

Jordan, Peter (1975), 'Librarians and social commitment', *Assistant Librarian*, **68**(4), April.

Kennedy, Helena (1997), *Learning works: widening participation in further education*, Coventry: Further Education Funding Council.

Knowles, Malcolm (1990), *The adult learner: a neglected species*, 4th edn, Houston: Gulf.

Kunkel, Lilith R., Weaver, Susan M. and Cook, Kim N. (1996), 'What do they know?: an assessment of undergraduate library skills', *Journal of Academic Librarianship*, **22**(6), November.

'Lack of facilities referred to the national commission' (1996), *Library Association Record*, **98**(1), January.

Lancaster, John M. (1991), 'Personal security' in Quinsee, A. G. and McDonald, A. C. (eds), *Security in academic and research libraries*, Newcastle upon Tyne: University Library.

Lederman, Linda Costigan (1991), 'Fear of talking: which students in the academic library ask librarians for help?', *RQ*, Summer.

Library Association (1992), 'Library provision for franchised courses', *Library Association Record*, **94**(7), July.

Library Trends (1991), **39**(4) (Special issue on library services to extended campus students).

Lieven, M. (1989), 'Access courses after ten years: a review', *Higher Education Quarterly*, **43**(2), Spring.

Lifer, Evan St (1994), 'How safe are our libraries?', *Library Journal*, **119**(13), August.

Liu, Mengxiong (1995), 'Library services for ethnolinguistic students', *Journal of Educational Media and Library Services*, **32**(3).

Livesey, Suzanne and Fisher, Shelagh (1997), 'Included, equal and independent?', *Library Technology*, **2**(4), August.

McDowell, Elizabeth (1985), *Part-time students and libraries*, Newcastle upon Tyne: Newcastle upon Tyne Polytechnic Products Ltd.

McLeod, R. A. (1993), 'Overseas students in an academic library', *Focus*, **24**(1).

Mellon, C. (1986), 'Library anxiety: a grounded theory', *College and Research Libraries*, 47, March.

Mellon, C. (1988), 'Attitudes: the forgotten dimension in library instruction', *Library Journal*, 1 September.

Morris, David (1993), 'The business of franchising', *Journal of Further and Higher Education*, **17**(1), Spring.

National Committee of Inquiry into Higher Education (1997), *Higher education in the learning society* (The Dearing Report), London: HMSO.

Nicholls, Anne (1997), 'Towards new horizons', *The Guardian Higher Education*, 21 January.

O'Donohue, Simon, H'Orle, Paul and Aldridge, Barrie (1992), 'Mature students: counselling and guidance – a role for libraries and learning resources providers', *Learning Resources Journal*, 8(2).

Pateman, John (1996), 'A question of breeding', *Library Association Record*, **96**(7), July.

Shepherd, Roddie (1997), 'Academic sector', *Library Association Record*, **99**(5), May.

Sheridan, Jean (1986), 'Andragogy: a new concept for academic librarians', *Research Strategies*, 4(4), Fall.

Slade, Alexander L. (1991), 'Library support for off-campus and distance education programs in Canada: an overview', *Library Trends*, **39**(4), Spring.

Smith, David N., Scott, Peter and Mackay, Leslie (1993), 'Mission impossible? Access and the dash to growth in British higher education', *Higher Education Quarterly*, **47**(4), Autumn.

Tooby, Barbara (1995), 'Library services for disabled users at the University of the West of England', *SCONUL Newsletter* 4, Spring.

Tunstill, Cathy (1991), *Mature students and college libraries*, Norwich: Norwich City College.

Unwin, Lorna (1994), 'I'm a real student now: the importance of library access for distance learning students', *Education Libraries Journal*, 37(2).

Velleman, Ruth A. (1990), *Meeting the needs of people with disabilities: a guide for librarians, educators, and other professionals*, Phoenix: Oryx.

Wise, Michael (1988), 'Provision for overseas students', *U C and R Newsletter*, 24, March.

Wood, Frances, Ford, Nigel, Miller, David, Sobczyk, Gill and Duffin, Robert (1996), 'Information skills, searching behaviour and cognitive styles for student-centred learning: a computer-assisted learning approach', *Journal of Information Science*, 22(2).

Woodrow, Maggie (1993), 'Franchising: the quiet revolution', *Higher Education Quarterly*, **47**(3), Summer.

Yacci, Michael (1994), 'A grounded theory of student choice in information-rich learning environments', *Journal of Educational Multimedia and hypermedia*, **3**(3/4).

5 Subject communities

Academic staff and students are concerned primarily with the subjects they teach and study. Below the most senior management, university and college structures reflect this concern in their subject-based structures normally through faculties or schools, and below that through subject departments. Although there may be other independent sections such as research centres, they will normally be linked to departments or faculties since they rest uneasily outside a structure upon which resource allocations are based and through which senior management controls activities. Oxford and Cambridge Universities differ in that the colleges exist as independent, self-governing corporate bodies distinct from the university, with their own property and income.

The importance of links with industry and the professions has become more vital as institutions strive to provide the workers needed to support the economic well-being of the country. These links are most easily forged by subject-based structures with which industry and the professions can identify, and the similarity of academic structures supports the interaction of academics with similar interests in different institutions.

Although the support services of institutions may stand outside the academic structure, they are likely to be most effective if the academic structure can be mirrored in their internal structures. Economies of scale and the need for some central control require many of these services to have managers with institution-wide responsibilities. Libraries will normally have a person in charge, and larger institutions will also have senior managers with institution-wide responsibilities. As far as users are concerned, the post of Head of Reader Services has frequently been created to coordinate provision. An important function of senior management is to liaise with other senior managers. This activity has been referred to as 'boundary management' (Stewart 1982) because it involves the maintenance of good relations with those outside the unit who could affect its work, so that the minimum disturbance is caused to the unit. It includes both the building up of a network of useful contacts who can provide information and help, and political activities which influence those with the power to affect the unit, especially those responsible for the provision of resources. The Fielden Report (John Fielden Consultancy 1993, p.26) noted how 'the management of libraries is becoming complex both politically and technically in a time of declining resources and rapidly increasing demand', and that there is a need for skills to cope with these pressures. Services to users can depend a great deal upon the effectiveness of senior librarians' boundary maintenance activities.

Subject librarianship

Fielden (John Fielden Consultancy 1993, p.26) found a wide range of practice in the role of subject or information librarian. Some had little contact with academic staff but it is my view that subject librarians are the foundation upon which effective work with users rests. Because they share the subject interests of staff and students, they are immediately able to empathize with users, given the appropriate attitudes, knowledge and skills. The Head of Research at the Victoria and Albert Museum has stated precisely what is needed:

I think that a key way for libraries to meet the challenges of the next decade has to be found in closer collaboration with their academic colleagues who use these facilities as teachers, scholars and curators. In the teaching sphere especially relations have to be close and, I would suggest, formalised. (Greenhalgh 1994, p.14)

Drawing upon job descriptions employed by Manchester Metropolitan University and the recommendations of Fielden I suggest that there are a number of essential characteristics that librarians need to possess. Foremost is the need to be extremely knowledgeable about the courses and research in their subject area, not superficially but through in-depth knowledge of course and research objectives, content of courses, teaching methods, course structures and assessment systems. What amounts to a community profile (Morris 1996, p.166) of appropriate courses and departments needs to be compiled so that the information can be passed on to other staff. The most valuable source is the validation/course review documents which will contain most of the information listed. Librarians tend to concentrate on the reading lists which such documents contain at the expense of other information, but this should be avoided. In fact some booklists in submissions bear little resemblance to those issued to students during the course, and some contain so many items not in stock in the library that there is a suspicion that they have been compiled with other motives. Most submissions will contain course monitoring and validation reports as well as the reports of external examiners, but more recent ones need to be seen if validation/review was not recent. There should also be feedback from course, departmental and faculty meetings, and validation/review events including 'participation in academic audit and quality assurance initiatives' (John Fielden Consultancy 1993, p.26). The recommendations which resulted from research at Manchester

Metropolitan University (Slack 1993, pp.16–17) are fully supported:

Subject librarians should be full members of Course Committees and should receive all documentation produced. Faculty secretaries and administrative assistants should ensure that librarians receive notice of meetings, agenda items and minutes. It may be thought that librarians do not have sufficient time to attend so many meetings and sometimes this may be the case (as, equally, with members of teaching staff). However, the main role of the subject librarian is to support the work of the teaching departments and, in order to plan effectively, she will make it her business to attend such relevant meetings.

The research also drew upon policy statements of the institution which stated that resourcing matters should be addressed prior to validation/review events so that they did not become major issues at the events themselves. It was therefore recommended that subject librarians should be considered as suitable members of steering groups and validation panels supported by the observation that:

All librarians have a first degree and the majority also have postgraduate and post-experience qualifications, often at Master's level. Many have wide experience in their subject field and in several academic institutions. They are a valuable addition to the range of expertise in each Faculty; to make use of them in this way would enhance the integration between teaching departments and the Library. (Slack 1993, p.16)

Representation on these formal committees helps to build up contacts with academic staff and these need to be enhanced by informal liaison both in the library and outside. Subject librarians should become familiar faces in academic departments and need to become knowledgeable about the interests and expertise of individuals so that they can bring relevant information to their notice.

User education of academic staff, researchers and students is a most important task for the subject librarian. In many ways this distinguishes the academic librarian from the public librarian, as ability to find information should be part of the educational process. This task has increased in importance as the amount of electronic data in subject areas has increased and is highlighted by Fielden (John Fielden Consultancy 1993, p.26), who describes it as 'providing technical support for staff and students through advice on how to get to, and through, the electronic text and databases that are most relevant to the subject (. . . "tailored navigational support")'. In the new universities the amount and level of 'teaching' carried out by librarians has been a decisive factor in grading decisions where librarians have been placed either on administrative or academic scales. User education itself is discussed in more detail in Chapter 7.

Subject librarians also need to publicize and promote their services, including the production of educational material, in a range of formats, to inform staff and students about resources in their subject area. Publicity and promotion are covered in Chapter 8.

Subject librarians will spend a high proportion of their time selecting material in their subject areas. The knowledge gained about courses and research is linked with the librarian's knowledge of books and periodicals, audiovisuals and electronic materials in the subject area, and the use made of this material, all of which help them to make informed judgements about material purchase. Older universities have tended to depend more on academic staff in the selection of material, whilst in newer universities and colleges more of the selection is carried out by the librarians. It is desirable that it should be a joint effort, with each using their own expertise to build up collections and subscribe to the most relevant services.

A variety of views exists as to whether subject librarians should classify material in their subject area and provide entries for the library's database. This partly depends on whether technical service functions are centralized or devolved. Database entries will already exist for most common material, with individual libraries able to make their own adjustments where necessary. Other material may have to be separately classified and catalogued, and libraries with specialized collections will have more of this material. My own view is that subject librarians should focus firmly on service to users and avoid spending disproportionate amounts of time on traditional back-room work.

Thus they should spend part of their time on enquiry desks, carrying out 'tutorial work' with students and staff, and assisting with technical and access problems.

There are several areas of conflict about the work of subject librarians which need to be resolved if they are to achieve their full potential. One particular difficulty concerns the amount of administrative work which they should be expected to perform. Fielden describes the job as a 'daunting' one (John Fielden Consultancy 1993, p.26), so it would seem that there would be enough to do without managerial responsibilities. My experience has been, however, that it is dangerous to separate work with users outside the library from the service they receive in the library. Thus a librarian managing a site library would have some subject responsibilities but also be responsible for services provided in the library. He or she would be assisted by others with subject responsibilities who also would have administrative duties. This arrangement does call for a greater variety of skills, but can provide greater job satisfaction, especially as in-library use can be more easily seen in the context of needs created within academic departments.

Academic staff are usually happy to use the services of subject librarians if they know that they understand their subjects and what they are trying to achieve. Thus, all other things being equal, a librarian with a subject qualification should be better able to help staff, researchers and students involved with that subject. This does not mean that librarians without formal qualifications will be unable to cope, but they do need to work at it and if possible obtain a subject qualification, if only at a lower level. Libraries have traditionally found it difficult, for example, to recruit graduates in science and technology. The changing environment has, however, increased the demand for flexibility in library staff. Employing subject specialists in specific unchanging posts is becoming more difficult, and there is constantly the conflict between employing a person in a specialist post and the wider needs of the library service which increasingly requires staff to be moved around as contingencies demand. Sometimes it is desirable anyway to provide fresh challenges where a person is in a rut. The lesson for the future is likely to be that flexibility will be a priority in selection policies.

'There is increasing evidence of the importance of course related variables, particularly teaching and assessment methods, and individual learning styles on the information seeking behaviour of undergraduates' (Day and McDowell 1985, p.31). Different subject areas display differing characteristics which have consequences for librarians supporting them. A discussion of some broad subject areas will illustrate these differences. It is beyond the scope of this book to deal with the many more specific subject areas such as music, law or nursing, all of which have their own characteristics and even within these there are differences depending, for example, on whether a course is deliberately vocational or 'academic'. It is hoped, however, to show how an understanding of subject features can help subject librarians to provide effective services.

Art and design

The cultural differences among subjects manifest themselves in the approaches of teaching staff and in the objectives of courses. In art courses great emphasis is placed upon creativity and originality, with individualized/independent learning the norm. Day and McDowell (1985, p.33) found in their survey that 'students followed their own interests in their own way and took a high level of responsibility for their personal achievements' and Hodgson (1993, p.15), observing students on an enterprise project, in which they were designing the interior of a public house, noted that 'the development of the project was based on "creativity and innovation" i.e. the client did not want the students to base their ideas on any current interior designs, and therefore information searching mainly comprised looking at catalogues for inspiration, using personal contacts and developing originally thought out ideas'.

Day and McDowell (1985, p.33) found a marked lack of guidance from academic staff concerning information and resources. Even for dissertations involving a literature review, some received little guidance. Students often worked in groups, helping each other and sometimes asking for advice on information sources.

A feature of the art and design projects investigated by Hodgson (1993) was the range of information sources both in subjects and in location used by the students, with the library resources being just one of them. In a project to design a theatre in a particular locality students visited theatres, attended performances, studied Ordnance Survey maps, visited the local planning authority, visited local libraries to find geological maps and books on local history. In the University Library they read the *Encyclopedia Britannica* and carried out literature searches on the history and culture of theatre. Of course the University Library could have provided directional information to many of these sources, but it was emphasized that the onus was placed on the student to undertake independent information research.

In the history of art course investigated by Day and McDowell, by contrast, there was an emphasis on reading lists and set texts, as would be expected of more 'academic courses'. As Greenhalgh (1994, p.15) points out, the 'new art history' is also, at its best, seamlessly interdisciplinary and art students and teachers are heavily dependent on sources covering a very wide range of subjects.

Keeping up with trends and fashions is very important for art and design students. The heavy use made of magazines and, increasingly, of videos provides clear evidence of this. 'The importance of "creative browsing" as a method of finding information cannot be overemphasised' (Day and McDowell 1985, p.36). As expected, the students like an informal atmosphere and long opening hours so that they can call in whenever they feel like it.

Information technology is becoming increasingly important

for art students and teachers. Dempsey and Lennon (1994, pp.10–15), for example, have shown how the Internet can provide information on art from academic institutions, enthusiasts, commercial, public and civic institutions and nationally funded services, whilst Greenhalgh (1994, p.16) strongly believes that for the art scholar 'IT is the key to all our futures' and goes as far as to say that 'the difference between a productive scholar and an unproductive one can largely be found in the extent to which he or she embraces the available technologies'.

Humanities

There are problems in defining humanities but most lists would include religion, philosophy, music, literature, linguistics and history. Stone (1982) has provided a comprehensive review of the literature. Unlike scientists, humanities scholars tend to work alone with the individual's interpretation being paramount. Thus there is a reluctance to delegate research since 'the journey is as important as the destination, and an account of the journey is as important as a picture of the destination' (Stone 1982, p.295). There is a reluctance also to use librarians – 'Lack of trust in librarians does play a strong part as does basic ignorance of the fact that librarians can and often do this kind of searching if asked' (Smith 1980, pp.29–30). On the other hand great value is placed on personal contacts – 'exchange of material and ideas, both with other people in the same field and also with all sorts of people in other fields, was frequent, and these contacts were sought and welcomed as a means of obtaining and disseminating information' (Corkill and Mann 1978, p.56).

There is a liking for browsing in the humanities which provides a 'means of serendipitous interaction with the materials of research' (Stone 1982, p.295). In an area like history the teacher wants the students to know certain 'facts'. 'These don't change much and are readily retrieved from standard monographs and textbooks . . . the teacher then wants the students to think about both the facts themselves and, and what has been written about them by people used to handling this kind of material' (Smith 1980, p.27).

Books and journals are heavily used, with books being at least as important as journals since older, definitive works are as important as recent material, and older material can also be used for comparative purposes. Original documents are needed, including primary materials such as original scores, works of art, texts, manuscripts, recordings and original literary works. There is therefore a reluctance to support the discarding of material as proposed by the Atkinson Report (University Grants Committee 1976) and a need to have access to special collections wherever they are located.

'Humanists use information technology less than scientists and social scientists for communication (e-mail), bibliographic searching and storage, transmittal, and analysis of primary evidence' (Wiberley and Jones 1994, p.503). The reasons for this are said to be 'the difficulty of analyzing their evidence with readily available software, the rarity of coauthorship, and the abundance of references to the secondary literature in the monographs they read' (Wiberley and Jones 1994, p.504). There is plenty of evidence, however, of interest in the contribution that information technology can make to the humanities. For example, two international conferences have been held since 1990, with the second one providing a wealth of information on networking in the humanities (Kenna and Ross 1995). Deegan (1995, p.236), a speaker at the 1995 conference, describes graphically the virtuality of networking:

A medieval palaeographer examining a manuscript in the Bodleian Library in Oxford will be able to call up a manuscript in Vienna or Prague or New York on her computer screen and compare the scripts directly instead of having to rely on memory or photographs which may take months to arrive. It will also be possible to compare the manuscripts interactively with the guidance of scholars in two or more locations simultaneously. An art historian will be able to assemble the entire oeuvre of an artist even though the individual works are in many galleries all over the world. Textual scholars will be able to search textbases without even being aware of where the individual texts reside in the virtual universe.

Social sciences

The subjects normally included here are anthropology, economics, education, law, political science, psychology and sociology. More debatable inclusions are history and geography. As Slater (1988, p.227) points out, 'at various points of time quite different disciplines may be thought of as social sciences' and 'others may drop out of the social science frame for the time being, as environmental pressures and cultural philosophies dictate. Such alterations in field definition are of high relevance to those attempting to provide information for the social sciences.' As definitions fluctuate, so also does the terminology, which limits the utility of keyword retrieval systems. Line (1971, pp.62–3), following the major INFROSS study, comments on the range of the social sciences, with each user at a point on a continuum from 'hard' to 'soft' science.

The 'hard' social scientist exhibits a number of characteristics that have been found in science user studies, and is distinguishable in a number of ways from the 'softer' social scientist. The experimental psychologist and the econometrician are at opposite poles from the sociological and educational theorist.

Line (1971, p.50) found that the heaviest-used materials were books, periodicals, research reports and government publications. Whilst a 'soft' social scientist may be happiest browsing, the 'hard' social scientist, such as a law student, is more likely to know what he or she wants – 'a law report, a book, a chapter or an article. Taught course students have a heavy reading commitment which is dictated by their reading lists' (Tearle 1994, p.75). The most useful method of locating information was following up references in books and periodicals.

A high percentage of the INFROSS respondents used material

over 25 years old and only 4 per cent found the local bookstock adequate to their requirements. The 'harder' social scientists, particularly those with direct relationships to practitioners such as lawyers, social workers and local government officers, need up-to-date information.

Although the INFROSS study found a 50–50 split between conjunctive users and consecutive users, Slater (1988, p.232) found all her interviewees were conjunctive users who 'need to have a desk spread with many documents at the same time, to which they cross-refer, quickly extracting, collating and comparing data from a variety of sources'. There are consequences for closed and open access, so that browsing is made easier, and for the number of items that can be loaned at any one time.

Like humanities scholars, many social scientists prefer to do their own information searching, feeling that it might be difficult to provide precise instructions to others and fearing the loss of the serendipity value of searching – 'search delegation, in spite of time constraints, still revealed a fair amount of DIY ethos, as being part of the research ethos. The economist, for instance, felt that it was part of his proper professional expertise to do this for himself. Some innate mistrust of another's capacity to know what he wanted was evident' (Slater 1988, p.232). They also seem less than willing to trust librarians, but rather use the library 'primarily as a source for obtaining previously identified information but not as a resource to identify relevant information' (Folster 1995, p.89).

Social scientists do make heavy use of informal channels, discussing their work with colleagues in their own institutions and in others.

From her review of user studies Folster (1995, p.91) concludes that 'computerized services ranked very low in their importance'. Even in a recent study of ethnic studies scholars, which she cites, a reluctance was expressed to use databases in electronic formats. On the other hand, there is plenty of evidence that the 'harder' social scientists are making more use of information technology – 'Is information technology transforming law librarianship? Yes. Will it change the nature of what librarians do? Perhaps. But, information technology is also creating the challenges and opportunities that make the future exciting in many fields, none more so than law librarianship' (Danner 1996, p.207).

Science and technology

'Because science is a supposedly rational and logical exercise it is often assumed that the information-seeking behaviour of scientists will follow similar logical, rational lines' (Palmer 1991, p.105), but 'scientists are not "empty buckets"; they are individuals who not only collect, store, retrieve and use information, but also create it. Moreover, they behave differently towards information in different situations. Few scientists find information retrieval systems easy to use, whether manual or electronic' (ibid., p.106).

Ellis, Cox and Hall (1993) studied the information-seeking patterns of researchers in the physical and social sciences using interviews and grounded theory, and found no major differences between the two groups. Browsing, for instance, in which social scientists and humanities scholars indulge, was also used by physicists in the familiarization process when looking for information on topics new to them (Ellis, Cox and Hall 1993, p.361). Browsing is also employed for current awareness though scientists monitor journals whilst social scientists monitor books and journals.

Heavy use is being made of electronic communication by scientists and technologists. The speed of e-mail dissemination whatever the distance has meant that 'it is now beginning to replace preprint distribution' (Meadows and Buckle 1992, p.280) with 'automated versions of invisible colleges' being created.

Scientists normally work in groups and use personal contacts a great deal to obtain information: 'conferences, and face-to-face meetings generally, continue to be a popular form of communication, despite funding cutbacks' (Meadows and Buckle 1992, p.281).

Although the general view might be that scientists have replaced paper searching with electronic searching, the pattern appears more variable. Younger staff are generally more comfortable with information technology than the senior staff, who are more influential in determining change, and are more resistant (Meadows and Buckle 1992, p.285). Ellis, Cox and Hall (1993, p.366) observed that 'while some researchers have employed electronic means of identifying references this has usually only constituted a small part of their information activities', and this is confirmed by a number of other studies quoted by them. The point is made that 'there does appear to be increasing interest in the USA in electronic communication of research results'.

A major difficulty for the scientist is information overload as large amounts of information are made available through online searching and with the trend towards end-user searching. This is particularly the case for non-textual systems such as 'leading-edge' information systems (Philip 1995, p.193) which were directly accessed by 70 per cent of academic chemists surveyed in ten universities.

Selectivity in research funding has led to a still growing emphasis on publishing, usually in a journal, and the cost of journals has presented problems to the librarian trying to manage a budget. Indeed the cost of all types of science and technology material provides considerable difficulties when allocating budgets.

The problems caused by the lack of subject specialists with scientific qualifications is well illustrated by Meadows and Buckle (1992, pp.276–90), who found that the lack of subject knowledge by library staff was cited by several departments as a reason for not making use of online searches.

Subject communities and the library

There has been a multitude of user studies over the last 30 years or so. Until recently (Ellis, Cox and Hall 1993, pp.356–7) there has been little attempt at uniformity of methodology and a lack of theoretical underpinning which has made satisfactory comparison among subject areas difficult, but a number of themes have emerged from the discussion of subject similarities and differences.

Definitions of some subjects is difficult, and in many areas of study and research a wide range of formats and subjects is included, well beyond what might initially have been expected. This means that those with immediate access to large comprehensive collections are at an advantage. Subject librarians also cannot afford to limit themselves to preconceived notions of subject boundaries, and must have some knowledge of subject areas beyond their own specialisms.

All subjects need up-to-date information, although it is less important in non-vocational areas. Thus great importance is attached to the journal literature, and in the future information technology is sure to gain greater prominence. On the other hand all subjects except science require access to older material, thus creating space problems for many libraries.

Some of the accommodation problems should be relieved by the use of information technology but, in spite of all the IT hype and the mass of literature, much of it written by librarians and information scientists, user studies show that its actual use is still limited, even in science and technology. Subject librarians have therefore much to do by way of publicity and user education if information technology is to achieve its potential.

Librarians still need to be accepted and trusted by users, especially by academic staff, many of whom make greater use of colleagues and informal contacts to obtain information. In their guide to management research Easterby-Smith, Thorpe and Lowe (1991, p.145) express this as follows:

The single most important aspect of using a library is to establish a rapport with one or a number of these professionals and, once the contact has been established, never to let it lapse. The ability to do this effectively means that the researcher has a go-between – someone who can communicate with the library system on his behalf.

The essential duties of the subject librarian, discussed in this chapter, are designed to encourage such a rapport – essential if the library is to fulfil its potential.

References

Corkill, Cynthia and Mann, Margaret (1978), *Information needs in the humanities: two postal surveys*, Sheffield: Centre for Research on User Studies.

Danner, Richard (1996), 'The effects of information technology on law librarianship: an American perspective', *Law Librarian*, **27**(4), December.

Day, Joan and McDowell, Elizabeth (1985), 'Information needs and uses of art and design students', *Education Libraries Bulletin*, **28**(3), Autumn.

Deegan, Marilyn (1995), 'Networking and the discipline', in Kenna, Stephanie and Ross, Seamus (eds), *Networking in the humanities: proceedings of the second conference on scholarship and technology in the humanities held at Elvetham Hall, Hampshire, UK, 13–16 April, 1994*, London: Bowker-Saur.

Dempsey, Lorcan and Lennon, Ann (1994), 'Art and the internet: some notes on resources and trends', *Art Libraries Journal*, **19**(4).

Easterby-Smith, Mark, Thorpe, Richard and Lowe, Andy (1991), *Management research: an introduction*, London: Sage.

Ellis, David, Cox, Deborah and Hall, Katherine (1993), 'A comparison of the information seeking patterns of researchers in the physical and social sciences', *Journal of Documentation*, **49**(4), December.

Folster, Mary B. (1995), 'Information seeking patterns: social sciences', *Reference Librarian*, 49/50.

Greenhalgh, Paul (1994), 'The art library – a moving target', *Art Libraries Journal*, **20**(2).

Hodgson, Marianne (1993), *Information searching for the development of enterprising projects*, Manchester: Manchester Metropolitan University Library.

John Fielden Consultancy (1993), *Supporting expansion: a report on human resource management in academic libraries for the Joint Funding Councils' Libraries Review Group*, Bristol: Higher Education Funding Council for England.

Kenna, Stephanie and Ross, Seamus (1995), *Networking in the humanities: proceedings of the second conference on scholarship and technology in the humanities held at Elvetham Hall, Hampshire, UK, 13–16 April, 1994*, London: Bowker-Saur.

Line, Maurice B. (1971), 'The information uses and needs of social scientists: an overview of INFROSS', *Aslib Proceedings*, **23**(8), August.

Meadows, A. J. and Buckle, P. (1992), 'Changing communication activities in the British scientific communities', *Journal of Documentation*, **38**(4), December.

Morris, Beryl (1996), 'The way ahead' in Pinder, Chris and Melling, Maxine (eds), *Providing customer-oriented services in academic libraries*, London: Library Association.

Palmer, Judith (1991), 'Scientists and information 1. Using cluster analysis to identify information style', *Journal of Documentation*, **47**(2), June.

Philip, G. (1995), 'Use of "leading-edge" information systems by academic chemists in the UK: part 1. The results of a preliminary investigation', *Journal of Information Science*, **21**(3).

Slack, Frances (1993), *The library and academic departments: final report*, Manchester: Manchester Metropolitan University Library.

Slater, Margaret (1988), 'Social scientists' information needs in the 1980s', *Journal of Documentation*, **44**(3), September.

Smith, Carole (1980), 'Problems of information studies in history' in Stone, Sue (ed.), *Humanities information research: proceedings of a seminar; Sheffield 1980*, Sheffield: Centre for Research on User Studies.

Stewart, Rosemary (1982), *Choices for the manager: a guide to managerial work and behaviour*, London: McGraw-Hill.

Stone, Sue (1982), 'Humanities scholars: information needs and uses', *Journal of Documentation*, **38**(4), December.

Tearle, Barbara (1994), 'Information strategies in the academic law library', *Law Librarian*, **25**(2), June.

University Grants Committee (1976), *Capital provision for university libraries: report of a working party* (The Atkinson Report), London: HMSO.

Wiberley, Stephen and Jones, William G. (1994), 'Humanists revisited: a longitudinal look at the adoption of information technology', *Colleges and Research Libraries*, **55**(6), November.

6 Researchers

Erens's (1991) survey of academics in higher education found that 49 per cent considered research as their primary activity compared with 29 per cent who considered teaching as their primary activity and 20 per cent who considered them equal. Eighty per cent had had some professional writing published in the last two years. Research was a greater priority in the older universities and this is borne out by the 1996 research assessment exercise (Research assessments 1996, pp.i–xvi) carried out by the Higher Education Funding Council. In both the 1992 and 1996 exercises Oxford and Cambridge Universities topped the ranking lists and both selected over 90 per cent of their academic staff for assessment whereas the new universities selected much smaller proportions and were graded much lower. The top new university, Sheffield Hallam, ranked sixtieth in 1996, selected 28 per cent of its staff, and had an average score of 3.56 on a 7-point scale compared with Oxford's 6.67. Most of the new universities, which acquired their current status following the Further and Higher Education Act 1992, have tried to increase their involvement with research, often from a low base, and the 1996 figures show that big improvements have been made by a number of them. In England the numbers of active researchers had risen by 45 per cent in the new universities since the previous exercise in 1992, compared with 5 per cent in old universities.

Research policy

This trend has led to debates about future research policy. On the one hand there is the view that research funding should be concentrated on those with high ratings – a super-league of five star research institutions. This view is held not only because it is thought that it would improve research but also because, as Webster (1997, p.12) puts it, 'the process [the research assessment exercise] corrupts the entire system of higher education by encouraging all to participate . . . the university system has gone research mad in recent years. In the process it has taken us further away from our students.' On the other hand it can be strongly argued that research can enhance the teaching, as the students will be close to those on the frontiers of knowledge. That depends, of course, on whether research takes staff away from teaching and whether researchers are necessarily good teachers. The fact is that there are funds to be gained from the research assessment exercise, since 97 per cent of the HEFC's money is distributed on the basis of the results, with the higher gradings receiving the most money and gradings of 1 and 2 receiving no funds. A notable feature of the 1996 results has been the performance of the plate-glass universities of the 1960s which suggests that the new universities could reasonably aspire to much higher ratings in the future.

Finance

In addition to the funds provided by HEFC, a variety of external bodies are used to finance research. In Erens's survey research councils provided funds to 44 per cent of those who said they were receiving external funding, 39 per cent of them received funds from commercial sponsorship, 38 per cent from central or local government and 23 per cent from research foundations (Erens 1991, p.20). Library and information services do have a role in providing information on possible sources of income. For example, valuable information on European funding is provided by Collins (1991) and the Department of Trade and Industry (Great Britain. Department of Trade and Industry 1996).

The work of the researcher

Finch and North (1991) carried out in-depth interviews with researchers who described the process of conducting their research. Research is characteristically a mix of ideas and exploratory thought with rigorous and systematic testing. The manner in which the research was undertaken and the material used differed considerably among subject areas. Research in history is characterized by the use of archival material and 'lots of looking up'. Original research requires the examination of original material and considerable travel may be necessary in order to consult it. The need to work at it continuously and to be able to obtain material quickly is paramount: 'It's vital that you follow up your references quickly. There's nothing like having a trail of cold references. You think "My God what did I want to look that up for?" The flash of inspiration which was there has gone cold' (Finch and North 1991, p.9). By contrast mathematics research is characterized by abstract thought and calculation – lots of sitting and thinking. 'For several mathematicians, the importance of journal articles as providing the raw material for their research was emphasised, and equated with the applied scientists' laboratory equipment/materials' (Finch and North 1991, p.1). In science and technology the emphasis is upon team-based laboratory work and it is essential to know what research has already been carried out and to be up to date.

Research proposals

Initially the vast majority of researchers who are requesting funds/time will have to write a proposal. Researchers may consider it as a nuisance which prevents them getting on with the research but Moore (1987, p.70) is firmly of the belief that 'the preparation of a proposal is an invaluable aid to the planning of the overall project. The discipline imposed by having to set down thoughts on paper ensures that all the stages are considered and allowance is made for every eventuality.' There are many guides such as Moore's which can help with the preparation of a proposal. Libraries should also be able to supply information which can be used to support an application, such as recent reports which make suggestions about the need for more knowledge in an area.

Proposals will also require applicants to state aims and objectives, the perceived value, methods to be used and also the relationship of the research to existing knowledge. Once the research is under way a thorough review of existing literature is normally an initial task for the researcher:

every research project in the social sciences should involve the inquirer in searching out previous, related investigations. Without this step, an integrated comprehensive picture of the world cannot be built. Researchers working in isolation repeat past mistakes and rarely achieve a sense of progress. Progress in social science comes from building on the efforts of those who have worked before. (Cooper 1989, p.7)

Leedy (1989, pp.66–7) goes further in listing the benefits of literature review:

1. It can reveal investigations similar to your own, and it can show you how the collateral researchers handle these situations.
2. It can suggest a method of dealing with a problematic situation that may also suggest avenues of approach to the solution of similar difficulties you may be facing.

3. It can reveal to you sources of data that you may not have known existed.
4. It can introduce you to significant research personalities of whose research efforts and collateral writings you may have had no knowledge.
5. It can help you to see your own study in historical and associational perspective and in relation to earlier and more primitive attacks on the problem.
6. It can provide you with new ideas and approaches that may not have occurred to you.
7. It can assist you in evaluating your own research efforts by comparing them with related efforts done by others.

The role of the library in the provision of this information is clear, but also there is a very important user education role in enabling researchers to search the literature systematically.

Libraries and researchers

Libraries are considered important by all researchers. Erens (1991, pp.23–86) found that 95 per cent of academic researchers considered access to a convenient well-stocked library as important or very important. Most regarded libraries in their own institution as most important for research, but where other libraries were mentioned it was usually those with 'more suitable collections' and they were mentioned more often by respondents from new universities. In addition there was greater use of other libraries than five years ago, particularly where collections were perceived to have deteriorated in their own institutions. These findings have a bearing upon recommendations made in the Anderson Report (*Joint Funding Councils' Library Review 1996*) on the need for institutions to publish information plans which will enable working relationships to be built up, and collection and retention responsibilities to be shared, and efforts thereafter, to find a way of compensating libraries which provide services to external users. Researchers are generally agreed that a good book and journal collection is vital, with journals considered especially important. Hence the concern expressed about the deterioration of journal collections as prices increase and large numbers of new journals are published.

The fact that research money has been obtained does not necessarily mean that money is available for the library. Erens found 'no evidence that books and journals were now more likely to be purchased through research grant money; in fact, some research grants expressly forbid the purchase of books and journals with grant money' (Erens 1991, p.45).

Access to materials not available in libraries' own stocks has thus become an even greater necessity. The inter-library loans service is therefore crucial, and in the future such access is increasingly likely to be through electronic means. Even in the early 1990s Erens found positive responses to questions about services such as online searches and information retrieval systems (Erens 1991), in contrast to concerns expressed about collections.

There is inevitably some conflict between library provision for teaching and provision for research. Generally speaking, journals are more commonly used by researchers whereas books, particularly key texts, are in greater demand by students. In 1996 the library at Manchester Metropolitan University obtained £250,000 to support research activities, and one of the uses made of the funding was to purchase some new journal titles and also to provide improved access to materials through increased support for the inter-library loans service and online searching. Additional CD-ROMs were also purchased. There was, too, an awareness that the hard-pressed subject librarians were finding it difficult to contact researchers as often as they should, especially with the higher profile being achieved by research in the institution. The solution lay in the appointment of two research support librarians on senior staff grades.

Like most such posts, these were used to coordinate the library's research support and to provide a link with the university's specialist support. In this case liaison with the university's Research Development Office and faculty research committees was an essential part of the job, especially to gain knowledge of both existing and proposed research and to feed back the information to subject librarians. Just as the library may be forgotten when plans for new courses are being formulated, so the necessary support of the library may be overlooked when proposals for research are being discussed. Recommendations in the Anderson Report (*Joint Funding Councils' Library Review: Report 1996*) show an awareness of this problem:

The Funding Councils should require that institutions' information strategies provide detail on how the institutions intend to secure adequate access to library material for research in the various subject areas in which they claim to be active.

In order to ensure that institutions have satisfactory arrangements for library support for their research, the Funding Councils should require that a summary of how library support is to be provided for an area of assessment is presented as part of an institution's submission in the Research Assessment Exercise. In addition the Research Councils, British Academy and other sponsors of research and postgraduate students, should, in considering the award of fellowships and studentships, assure themselves that proper library support will be available.

If these recommendations are adopted, institutions will have to look more carefully at library provision when research proposals are being examined internally so that difficulties do not arise when external assessments are carried out.

To discover the real needs of researchers at Manchester Metropolitan University, focus groups were set up and a questionnaire survey of researchers and research assistants was carried out. User education was deemed to be a priority, and research seminars were conducted to publicize the support the library was able to give, with an emphasis on how to search electronically and how to use bibliographic software such as Papyrus. Further publicity was provided by the production of guides for researchers, including an introduction to the Internet and a pamphlet on bibliographical citation.

These activities underline the increasing importance of information technology to the researcher. Commentators such as

Brown (1993, pp.42–3), however, have noted that many researchers still depend largely on 'interpersonal discussions' and printed sources (Collins 1991), and the Anderson Report concludes that there are so many legal and cultural obstacles to the electronic approach that, in the short term, it would not be a feasible base for a research strategy. In the longer term, however, it seems inevitable that material for researchers will increasingly be available in digital form. 'It is possible to envisage that one day most formal communication of research results currently done through journals and conference proceedings might be done on computer networks' (Breaks 1993, p.99).

Teaching needs of lecturers

There are many incentives for academic staff to engage in research, and figures quoted above show that many consider it their primary activity. The Committee of Scottish University Principals (Macfarlane 1992, p.ix) is not happy with this state of affairs in higher education and considers that 'the greatest challenge is to persuade a majority of those involved in higher education to see teaching as their prime activity, and as one posing intellectual challenges and offering rewards comparable to those of standard research'. Involvement in research is desirable for lecturers as it helps to keep them in the forefront of knowledge and up to date. The information needs of lecturers and researchers therefore overlap to a certain extent. Experience as a lecturer has made me aware of some of the differences, however. Researchers tend to have more time to contemplate their work and, though panic can set in as deadlines approach, this is not quite the same as needing a piece of information for a lecture beginning in one hour's time. Lecturers also need material that can be used with students as teaching aids. Thus audiovisual material is becoming more important, with increasing amounts being relevant to further and higher education. Libraries which have converged with educational technology support services will also find themselves involved with the production of audiovisual material and with advice on its use.

Examples are needed to illustrate lectures or for use in seminars and tutorials. Some of these come under the category of grey or ephemeral material which is sometimes considered unsuitable for stocking by libraries and it is left to the lecturers themselves to collect it. For example, annual reports and balance sheets of companies for business students, publicity and promotion publications for art and design students, election literature for students of politics. My experience has been that the larger the library, the less it wants to be involved unless someone has taken a special interest and formed a 'special collection' which can emphasize preservation for the future rather than hands-on use by present-day students.

'Academics are all committed to keeping abreast of the latest research and ideas in their discipline, but few of them have the opportunity to keep at the forefront of developments in how to teach their subject' (National Committee of Inquiry into Higher Education 1997, p.31). As teaching methods change and active learning is encouraged, lecturers need information on teaching in further and higher education, with plenty of examples of good practice. Again some of the material may be looked on by librarians as too ephemeral and the awkward formats cause problems for those preferring everything to be in book-like form. More material of all types is becoming available on the Internet, and this will be a great help in the future.

Not only do lecturers need to keep up to date with their subjects and with teaching practice, but they also need to keep abreast of developments in the politics of education in their own institutions and outside. This is desirable as staff need to be aware of changes in their own environment and to be effective in their administration and management roles, which occupy them for 15 per cent of the time (30 per cent for professorial staff), according to the survey carried out for the Dearing Report (National Committee of Inquiry into Higher Education 1997, p.30). Journals, reports and internally produced documents such as committee minutes will provide for most of their needs, together with increasing amounts of information on the Internet. Other staff development activities such as those supporting academics' personnel and financial roles also need to be supported by the library.

A number of academic libraries provide written guidance for academic staff, both in printed form and on computer networks, recognizing that there is particular information which they need to know, and thus supporting a working partnership with them. In addition to the general information which everyone needs, such as how to join the library, how to borrow material, how to find material, how to use the catalogue, how to obtain items from other libraries, how to gain access to other libraries and the penalties for keeping material overdue, they need to know:

• the names and job titles of the senior staff responsible for the library service as a whole and those staff such as site librarians and subject librarians whose job it is to support their work;

• how the library can help with their own teaching and research;

• how to make suggestions for purchase of all types of material;

• about availability of rooms in the library which can be used by tutors, how they can be booked and any regulations which apply;

• about user education for themselves and their students, with particular emphasis on information technology;

• how to obtain access to materials the lecturer wants his students to use, for example, short loans, one-week loans and so on;

• how to make correct references to materials cited;

• about ways in which academic staff can make their views known about the library.

The guide is also an opportunity for the library to ask for help from lecturers and to point out some of the problems which the library has by:

• asking for help in ensuring the library is consulted well

before validation and review events and quality assessments;

- emphasizing the role of the library in support of active learning and the importance of using the library to its full potential, for example, by students consulting a range of materials and looking for information themselves;
- publicizing the problems the library has with security, vandalism and noise;
- explaining funding difficulties and why every request for purchase, especially those with continuing commitments, such as periodicals, cannot be met.
- explaining why there are inevitable delays between order and purchase.

The leaflet produced for new academic staff at Manchester Metropolitan University sums up the desirable relationship between the library and academic staff:

The Library exists to enable effective teaching, learning and research to take place in the University. It is not merely a support service but an essential part of the academic enterprise for both staff and students. For this to be a reality there has to be the closest liaison between Library staff and academic staff. A very high proportion of the tasks which students are set have consequences for the Library which are not always realised.

References

Breaks, Michael (1993), 'SuperJANET project on information resources (SPIRS): a study commissioned by the JNT' in *Libraries and IT: working papers of the Information Technology Sub-committee of the HEFCs' Libraries Review*, Bath: UKOLN (The Office for Library and Information Networking).

Brown, David (1993), 'Present status of electronic publishing within the UK publishing industry' in *Libraries and IT: working papers of the Information Technology Sub-committee of the HEFCs' Libraries Review*, Bath: UKOLN (The Office for Library and Information Networking).

Collins, Martin (1991), *A complete guide to European research technology and consultancy funds*, 2nd edn, London: Kogan Page.

Cooper, Harris M. (1989), *Integrating research: a guide for literature reviews*, 2nd edn, London: Sage.

Erens, Bob (1991), *Research libraries in transition: academic perceptions of recent developments in university and polytechnic libraries*, Boston Spa: British Library Research and Development Department (Library and Information Research Report 82).

Finch, Helen and North, Cathy (1991), *The research process: the library's contribution in times of constraint*, London: British Library Research and Development Department (British Library Research Paper 95).

Great Britain. Department of Trade and Industry (1996), *Telematics applications: a guide to writing successful proposals*, London: Department of Trade and Industry.

Joint Funding Councils' Library Review: Report of the group on national / regional strategy for library provision for researchers (The Anderson Report), (1996), OURL http://ukoln.bath.ac.uk./elib/wk—papers/anderson.html.

Leedy, Paul D. (1989), *Practical research: planning and design*, 4th edn, London: Collier Macmillan.

Macfarlane, A. G. J. (1992), *Teaching and learning in an expanding higher education system*, Edinburgh: SCFC.

Moore, Nick (1987), *How to do research*, 2nd edn, London: Library Association.

National Committee of Inquiry into Higher Education (1997), *Higher Education in the learning society* (The Dearing Report), London: HMSO.

'Research assessments 1996' (1996), *Times Higher Education Supplement*, 1259, 20 December.

Webster, Frank (1997), 'Pros and cons of a super league', *Times Higher Education Supplement*, 1261, 3 January.

7 User education

User education has had a mixed reception over the years. On the one hand, there are those who believe it is the most important role of the library in an educational institution. On the other, there are the critics who view it as an optional extra – a teaching function which conflicts with the organization and preservation functions at the core of librarianship. The plea in this book is for the library to be seen as an integral part of the educational enterprise so that librarians and academics can work together to enhance learning and not be jealously guarding each other's territories. It is my experience that librarians possess an immense knowledge of the literature in their subject areas because they are dealing with that literature every day. In many cases this knowledge is superior to that held by most academics. Of course there are exceptions, but academic librarians are only too familiar with outdated book-lists and ignorance of new sources available through information technology.

Aims of user education

A major aim of user education is therefore to widen the use of a range of library resources which will enable academics to improve their teaching and research and students to improve their learning and achieve better results in their work. In both cases success depends upon rewards being given for the extra effort being made through, for example, course audits and student assessments. Master's account of user education at the University of Nevada at Las Vegas brings this out very well as 'both the reference staff and instructional staff knew that graduate students would make more intense use of library resources for coursework and assignments only if they were encouraged by their professors and if they saw how these resources held value for them' (Master 1995, p.117). This view is also strongly reinforced by Baker's summary of studies since the 1960s, which have found library use to be 'most often driven by faculty demand' . . . but 'teaching faculty do not hold the expectation of student library use that librarians do. This is despite the fact that most of these faculty would probably support the values which are intrinsic to "information literacy" ' (Baker 1995, p.378).

Many librarians seek to justify user education as a means of reducing pressure on enquiry desks by enabling users to find information for themselves. It is very difficult to test the validity of this argument, since users will certainly be in a better position to initiate a search, but they will inevitably meet problems which they will be unable to solve by themselves. Users need not only to be able to access information but also to evaluate it, and synthesize it. Traditionally the first need is largely the library's responsibility, whilst academic staff are seen as being most concerned with evaluation and synthesis, but it should be a joint enterprise. Librarians are too often unwilling to contribute to the evaluation and synthesis processes, although they may have important information on the value of items and on the relationship between one piece of information and another.

Over the last decade or so many academic institutions have formally recognized the need for guidance by the appointment of study skills staff, often as an arm of student services. It is sensible for the library to be associated with this trend for, in addition to the objectives already discussed for user education, study skills also cover such areas as organizing oneself for study, reading effectively, note making, writing, taking part in group work and seminars, and examination technique.

User education affords a great opportunity for introducing the library staff to the users. In particular the subject specialists most responsible for supporting courses can be introduced to those teaching and studying those courses. From the induction phase onwards users should be able to identify library staff who can help them most.

Librarians also have to be aware that the efforts made in user education contribute both positively and negatively to the image of the library in the mind of the user. Although this is true of everything the library does, it is especially so where the library goes out to meet the user.

Information technology

Developments in higher education, described in Chapter 1, have greatly influenced user education in Britain. Cowley and Hammond's 1987 summary, quoted in Harris's valuable survey of user education and user studies (Harris 1993, pp.170–91) is still broadly an accurate description:

The time and opportunity for librarians to plan and develop effective education programmes appears to have declined in recent times. Resource difficulties in further and higher education have forced library staff into partial retreat as the main pre-occupation has been that of defending basic services. The scope for the more exploitative forms of activity has declined as staffing levels have decreased. Libraries have been busier and more heavily used as student numbers have increased and styles of teaching have changed. The demands of new technology have absorbed resources to an unforeseen extent and seized the imagination of senior library staff who might otherwise have spent more time on user contact services. (Cowley and Hammond 1987, p.34)

Although the introduction of the new technology has diverted resources away from traditional user education activities, it has also provided a lifeline. It has to be admitted that a good deal of user education which concentrated necessarily on printed materials, especially when they were talked about rather than handled, has been boring for students and felt to be unnecessary by academic staff, whether justified or not. Keyboard searching is far more attractive to most students; so much so that two writers from California State University Library are able to state that:

Students do not fear technology, but instead ascribe almost magical powers to it. If something is not found in a paper source it does not exist. The computer is synonymous with the information it accesses and is unimpeachable. A high percentage of learners will steadfastly resist any attempt to persuade them to use a printed source even when no exact computer equivalent exists. To-day's students want answers and are impatient with complex retrieval of information. To-morrow's students will be more so. To-day's learners have experienced new entertainment media that use multimedia and electronics to provide stunning visual effects and a rapid pace. Will they not expect as much in their information environment? (Dusenbury and Pease 1995, p.100)

Academic staff are aware that they cannot be expected to know about the latest information technology sources and are therefore motivated to learn, especially where institutional IT initiatives and rewards are in evidence. User education is becoming so dominated by information technology that the term 'information literacy' is being adopted, especially in the United States, since it is believed that 'the term and concept of library user education are not sufficient to carry the profession into the electronic age' (Tiefel 1995, pp.318–38).

In the same way that IT has been seen as a valuable aid to teaching in an age of scarce resources, so it is increasingly being used in the education of users. Hopkins (1995, pp.16–17) found that

> in comparison to the 1991/2 CTILIS survey, when only seven libraries were using either commercial or in-house computer-based tutorial packages for some aspect of user education training, this survey found that 31 libraries were using such packages. Of these 31, twenty were in-house developments. This compares to only three indicated in the 1991/2 survey, an increase of 670%.

A survey by Furner-Hines and Willett (1995, pp.23–32) found a good deal of use of the World Wide Web by UK academic libraries in the provision of home-page user guidance, and an eLib project at the University of Sheffield is aimed at supporting librarians in higher education in 'their development of the professional practice of NLS [networked learner support], in terms of helping them to take informed decisions about transferring some of their user support into the networked environment' (Levy, Fowell and Worsfold 1996, pp.34–5).

The development of information technology in higher education has been encouraged by a number of initiatives, including the Information Technology Training Initiative and the Teaching and Learning Technology Programme. The latter programme, for example, funded computer-assisted learning packages at Glasgow University Library using hypertext and hypermedia (Creanor and Durndell 1994, pp.349–65). Programmes under this funding have the additional advantage of having to be made available for a nominal charge to all other institutions supported by the UK Higher Education Funding Councils. IT packages enable users to pace the learning according to their own needs and convenience, the information provided is consistent, and staff are released for other professional duties. A good example of an induction package is Liverpool John Moores University's *Infopoint*, an interactive self-instruction package on using the library, which employs multimedia to show plans of floors and photographs (Gorman and Lees 1995, pp.85–94). There are plans in Liverpool to produce similar specialist guides to OPAC, BIDS (Bath Information and Data Services) and CD-ROM. Perhaps the most spectacular developments have been training sessions on the Internet itself. Richard Smith at the University of Southwestern Louisiana ran two sessions on 'Navigating the Internet' and attracted 865 participants in his first workshop and more than 12,000 in the second (Page and Kesselman 1994, pp.157–67). Another example of the way things are likely to progress can be seen in the work of Peritas, ICL's training subsidiary, which offers a range of online technical courses on which anyone with access to the World Wide Web can enrol – a virtual classroom. Students 'work at their own pace . . . Each student is assigned a tutor to monitor progress and answer questions' (Shaikh 1996, p.21).

The self-explanatory library

The development of user instruction packages that can be used without an intermediary can be viewed as part of a general philosophy espousing the *self-explanatory library* 'in which library users, when and as they need to do so, acquire library skills simply by using the library: all is explained; everything is transparent; skills are learned by doing which is facilitated by clearly articulated instructions' (Pacey 1995, pp.95–104). Pacey advocates a library which has effective signs and guiding, a range of well-produced printed guides and leaflets, self-instruction workbooks, on-demand multimedia packages to explain services, menu-driven user-friendly computer systems, with suitable point-of-use instructions, but also staffed enquiry points and accessible subject librarians who can deal with problems which will inevitably arise. Librarians have frequently been accused of designing unnecessarily complicated systems which are not planned sufficiently with users in mind and which therefore require librarians to explain them:

A great deal of time and effort can be devoted to instructing library users in basic library use, by lectures, seminars, audiovisual guides and other devices of greater or lesser sophistication.

This effort would in many cases be better spent on designing catalogues and libraries for ease of use. Some libraries are guilty of designing instructional courses to guide users through complexities of the libraries' own devising. (Line 1974, pp.383–91)

Gorman (1990, pp.354–62) quotes the words of Groucho Marx (as Rufus T. Firefly in 'Duck Soup') when warning of another pitfall which must be overcome if truly user-friendly systems are to be created:

Minister of Finance: Your Excellency, here is the Treasury Department's report. I hope you'll find it clear.
Firefly: Clear? Huh! Why a four year old child could understand this report. [Long pause as he studies it.] Run out and find me a four year old child. I can't make head or tail out of it.

The danger is, of course, that we will make systems that seem simple *to us* and will ignore the way the system appears to others. Send for a child of four.

User education activities

Most libraries divide user education into two major activities: induction and more detailed education, often subject-related. Induction usually takes place at the beginning of the academic year. It is therefore crammed in with other activities and library staff are heavily involved over a short period of time. Inexperienced staff, unused to speaking to large groups, can find the experience daunting, though the premonitions are normally worse than the event itself. Cowley's survey (Cowley 1988) identified the problems common in induction, and these are drawn upon in the discussion which follows, together with the findings of research carried out by Judith Andrews at Manchester Metropolitan University (Andrews 1990). Solutions to these problems have to be sought when planning induction programmes if they are to be effective.

Induction

This area of work necessitates a social action approach in which the librarian enters the perceptions of the user. Too often inductions can consist of a prepared programme which takes little account of the recipient's position. Students will be unable to absorb a great deal of information at a time when their priorities will often include finding and settling into their accommodation, sorting out timetables, meeting fellow students and collecting grants. Therefore induction must be short and concentrate upon the absolute basics. Good teaching also takes account of users' existing knowledge, expectations and information-searching habits. Atkinson and Scott made use of these concepts in the delivery of courses to Access students at Hackney Community College. Sessions began with the students working in small groups, identifying what they expected the library to do for them (Atkinson and Scott 1995, pp.45–8). Yacci's research (Yacci 1994, pp.327–50) on students' choice of resources has shown that a variety of approaches are chosen by students and that information services should allow for the different approaches. User education can easily suggest that there is only one best way to search for information. For example, many students want a broad conceptual structure for information, then to follow it with additional learning resources, whilst others prefer to 'dive in at the deep end' of the task and then seek resources later.

Because it takes place early, induction creates an image of the library which is difficult to change. Therefore it is most important that the presentation is effective and that any printed material given to the user is of a high quality. Judith Andrews, for example, found that a tape-slide presentation had to be replaced by a sophisticated video. The take-away material should lead the user towards more sophisticated use of the library and contribute to the idea of the self-explanatory library. Although many libraries include tours of the library as a major element in induction, it is a dubious practice, not least because it appears to remove the onus from the users to find their own way round the library with the help of explanatory systems. Additionally, tours are often extremely disruptive to other users.

The increased use of computer-based tutorial packages is contributing to the self-explanatory library, with many of those listed by Hopkins (1995) and Furner-Hines and Willett (1995) consisting of introductory guides to the library. Many libraries also make use of workbooks which students can take away and work through themselves. The workbooks can be self-marked or a computerized system can be used to assess multi-choice questions. Should a stage be reached where induction can be carried out without intermediaries, a decision has to be made on the importance of using induction to introduce library staff to users. My own belief is that this is still a most important function of the induction process.

Cowley found that librarians often had trouble with the administration of induction. There was failure to keep to agreed timetables, tutors would require the library to deal with excessively large groups, and there were too many last-minute requests. Although it would be difficult to eliminate all these problems, they could all be alleviated by improved liaison between the library and the tutors, not merely at induction time but throughout the year, so that each is aware of the other's objectives and difficulties, and so that to transgress would be like deceiving a friend. One significant indicator of this liaison which is visible to students is the presence of academic staff at induction sessions. It can be easily understood why tutors might welcome a break during a very busy period, but their attendance also improves attendance by the students, especially at the end of the day when the temptation to slip off home is greatest.

For both the library and the academic departments it is most important that senior management is supportive to user education. There is little worse than knowing that senior managers believe what you are doing is marginal.

The teachable moment

More detailed user education should take place when motivation is at its height – what Dusenbury and Pease call 'the
teachable moment . . . the optimal time when a learner is ready
to learn' (Dusenbury and Pease 1995, p.101). They instance the
teachable moments at the enquiry desk when the librarian
answers the articulated question and seeks to impart the gen-
eralizability of this situation to future questions. Ironically such
'mini lectures' are what earlier library education aims to avoid.
It is also often evident that students are satisfied with the answer
to the query itself rather than with how to answer such queries
in the future. Another teachable moment is when information
searching needs to take place to support an assignment. As far
as students are concerned, the need is likely to be subject-related
and therefore carried out by a subject librarian, where such
posts exist. Cowley has produced some valuable guidelines for
success and these will be used as a basis in the discussion that
follows.

Involvement with academic staff

The involvement of academic colleagues in user education is
vital both in the education of academic staff themselves and in
the education of the students they teach. Breaks (1993, p.89),
writing about the use of SuperJANET, describes a common
situation which has to be changed if the majority of academic
staff are to benefit from the new technology:

At the present time many of these resources have remained
the province of the networking 'expert' within each academic
department, who sometimes guards the information from lesser
mortals, but the demands on these services are increasing and
there are not enough of the 'experts' to deal with user demands.
Training is required to allow the non computer-literate user of
the network to become confident in using computers and
thence the network.

Where relationships with academic staff are strong and continuous, knowledge of what each is doing and planning will be regularly communicated. Thus academics will be aware of the library's induction programme and its content and may well have been involved in its planning. They will therefore be able to build upon it in their own courses. Similarly, there should be close consultation when more detailed subject-related user education takes place. The most successful of these programmes have been when information searching has been integrated into the course, with assessments set and marked by librarians. Even better, because more integrative, is to include an element in the assessment of an assignment which covers information searching and sources used. Frank Hatt, writing some time ago, articulates my own view perfectly:

What is really needed is for the development of library-based independent learning skills to be built into the course, along with the development of other learning skills . . . building library skills into the course is not just a matter of giving a librarian a slot on the timetable. It is a matter crucially of making a librarian a member of the course team and involving the whole course team in the determination of the course's aims and objectives and how they are to be met. (Hatt 1978, p.14)

Such involvement is likely to require an increasing amount of librarians' time so that, at present and for the foreseeable future, decisions need to be made on priorities and on methods of reducing the time without affecting quality, especially through the application of IT and self-teaching systems.

It is also a considerable advantage if an endorsement can be given at a high level, whether by a department, a faculty or by an institution as a whole. Master, for example, highlights the importance at the University of Nevada, Las Vegas, of obtaining an endorsement from the Dean of Libraries, the Faculty Senate, the governance body and the University Library Committee (Master 1995, pp.115–29). The Hollings Faculty of the Manchester Metropolitan University passed a resolution that students on all courses must receive user education.

Presentation skills

Although the use of self-teaching systems is increasing rapidly, there is still room for human contact with users, particularly where introducing staff to users is considered important. It follows therefore that ability to teach should be taken into account when recruiting and selecting staff, especially subject librarians. Although many schools of librarianship provide students with some practice at speaking to groups, my own experience is that all of them need more training in presentation skills. Micro-teaching, for example, is a feature of in-service training at Manchester Metropolitan University where speaking to groups, handling questions and discussion groups is considered important for all new professional staff, since increasingly staff need to be flexible as there are fewer fixed posts, even at subject librarian level. Like most successful user education, it is highly practical and interactive. Participants make presentations individually and these are each discussed by the group so that they learn from each other. This approach is sympathetic to the learning theory of 'andragogy' – the art and science of helping adults, which adopts a progressive and behavioural philosophy of education. Knowles (1990) has long been a proponent whose andragogical model provides valuable guidelines for librarians teaching adults. Its main assumptions are that adults need to know why they need to learn something before undertaking to learn it. They have a concept of being responsible for their own decisions and need to be treated by others as capable of self-direction. They have accumulated more experience than younger people, and this experience should be tapped into through experiential techniques. Adults become ready to learn those things they need to know to cope with their real-life situations, and are motivated to learn something to the extent that they perceive that it will help them to perform tasks and deal with problems.

Evaluation

Lack of adequate evaluation has long been seen as a major weakness in user education. Harris (1993, p.174) believes Cowley to be 'spot on' in his assessment:

The lack of evaluation of information skills teaching is a serious weakness in the case of any increase in this activity. The library needs to assess the value, results and intellectual underpinning of its work if a stronger case is to be made. There needs to be a setting of objectives, consideration of content and a willingness to revise or review teaching methods in the light of learning theories and wider academic developments. (Cowley 1987, p.31)

This criticism does seem to have had an effect, as Hopkins found in 1995 that 92 per cent of respondents had tried to evaluate their user education programmes, 40 per cent more than in 1991/92. Most librarians evaluate informally through noting the reaction of students, and some feel that is the best and most unobtrusive method, but more formal methods are required if the evaluation is meant to improve quality. Formal evaluation is therefore necessary and is concerned with the reaction of the participants, the learning that has taken place and the performance of the participants after the programme. Reaction is concerned with the views of the participants during and immediately after the programmes. This can be carried out through questionnaires and oral discussion with individuals or groups. The checklist shown on p.129–30 from Jordan (1995, p.182–3) takes into account the features in an oral presentation which require evaluation and can be used by library staff or be adapted as a questionnaire for completion by participants. What has been learned can be evaluated through written or oral tests and workbooks, which are now a feature of many user education programmes. Performance beyond the programme itself can be tested as part of course assessments, as described earlier in this chapter, or specific follow-ups might be carried out such as asking students a few weeks after attending an Internet training course 'what they have done on the network and what they found useful. Another option is to ask users to record Internet sessions in a diary or log for a set period of time, along with comments on their experiences' (Page and Kesselman 1994, p.163).

Successful evaluation depends upon a clear understanding of aims and objectives. The main aims of user education have already been discussed at the beginning of this chapter. The need to have users and their perceptions firmly in mind, the major theme of this book, is especially important when specific objectives are being defined for training sessions. This is well illustrated by Makulowich, writing about the teaching of Internet, when he stresses the need to match objectives to the composition of the class and to student interests (Makulowich 1994, pp.27–30) and by Scott (1994, pp.305–10), who emphasizes the importance of making 'each talk individual to the group being addressed . . . Some people may be more knowledgeable than the trainer about Internet; others may have heard the word Internet mentioned in their Sunday paper or on a television programme.'

The aims of user education have been examined in this chapter. Information technology is being used to support these aims, both as a motivational factor and as a tool to be exploited. Like most other aspects of academic librarianship, user education should be carried out with the close cooperation of academic colleagues if it is to be successful, and its effectiveness needs to be evaluated frequently.

Checklist of features of a good presentation

Please *ring* the score for each feature. High scores for high achievement, e.g. ⑤.

OBJECTIVES
1   Audience made aware of the objectives of the presentation from the start in terms of what members should be able to achieve.

1   2   3   4   5

STRUCTURE
2   Audience clear about how the presentation is meant to proceed and what their role should be.

1   2   3   4   5

3   The presentation clearly followed the logical structure that had been outlined.

1   2   3   4   5

ARRANGEMENTS
4   Arrangements had clearly been made beforehand giving confidence that the presentation would proceed without foreseeable problems, e.g. seating arrangements, audiovisuals, timing . . .

1   2   3   4   5

LANGUAGE
5   The language was easily understood by the audience, e.g. non-jargon.

1   2   3   4   5

CONTENT
6   All points discussed were important ones. Less important/marginal ones left to discussion session.

1   2   3   4   5

METHOD
7   Held the interest of the audience the whole time.

1   2   3   4   5

PRESENTATION
8   The presentation had:
    (1)   Sufficient variety.

1   2   3   4   5

    (2)   Correct pace.

1   2   3   4   5

    (3)   Good voice delivery – easy to understand and 'kept up' at end of sentences.

1   2   3   4   5

(4)   Energy and enthusiasm.

1   2   3   4   5

(5)   Emphases which were appropriate.

1   2   3   4   5

(6)   No off-putting mannerisms.

1   2   3   4   5

(7)   No barriers between the audience and the presenter, e.g. presenter looked directly at audience, no unnecessary physical barriers.

1   2   3   4   5

(8)   Adaptations were made to the audience's response as the presentation proceeded.

1   2   3   4   5

AUDIOVISUALS
9   Audiovisuals were:
   (1)   Legible/audible.

1   2   3   4   5

   (2)   Fitted in well.

1   2   3   4   5

   (3)   Equipment worked.

1   2   3   4   5

HANDOUTS
10   Handouts were effective.

1   2   3   4   5

References

Andrews, Judith (1990), *Manchester Polytechnic Library: a study to investigate the effect and control of change in its internal and external environments*, Manchester: Manchester Polytechnic Department of Library and Information Studies.

Atkinson, Judy and Scott, Nicola (1995), 'Rethinking information skills teaching', *Learning Resources Journal*, **11**(2), June, pp.45–8.

Baker, Robert K. (1995), 'Working with our teaching faculty', *College and Research Libraries*, **56**(5), September.

Breaks, Michael (1993), 'SuperJANET project on information resources: a study commissioned by the JNT' in *Libraries and IT: working papers of the Information Technology Sub-committee of the HEFCs' Libraries Review*, Bristol: UKOLN.

Cowley, John (1988), *A survey of information skills teaching in UK higher education*, London: British Library (British Library Research Paper 47).

Cowley, J. and Hammond, N. (1987), *Educating information users in universities, polytechnics and colleges*, London: British Library (British Library Research Review 12).

Creanor, Linda and Durndell, Helen (1994), 'Teaching information handling skills with hypertext', *Program*, **28**(4), October.

Dusenbury, Carolyn and Pease, Barbara G. (1995), 'The future of instruction', *Journal of Library Administration*, **12**(3/4).

Furner-Hines, Jonathan and Willett, Peter (1995), 'The use of the World-Wide Web in UK academic libraries', *Aslib Proceedings*, **47**(1), January.

Gorman, Michael (1990), 'Send for a child of four! or creating the BI-less academic library', *Library Trends*, **39**(1&2), Summer/Fall.

Gorman, P. and Lees, R. (1995), 'Designing Infopoint: a multi-purpose multi media library guide', *The New Review of Academic Librarianship*, 1.

Harris, Colin (1993), 'User education and user studies' in *British librarianship and information work 1986–1990*, vol. 2, London: Library Association.

Hatt, Frank (1978), *Art Libraries Journal*, **3**(4), Winter.

Hopkins, Tracy (1995), *User education in academic libraries: results of the CTILIS survey 1995*, Loughborough: CTI Centre for Library and Information Studies, Department of Information and Library Studies, Loughborough University.

Jordan, Peter (1995), *Staff management in library and information work*, 3rd edn, Aldershot: Gower.

Knowles, Malcolm (1990), *The adult learner: a neglected species*, 4th edn, Houston: Gulf.

Levy, Philippa, Fowell, Sue and Worsfold, Emma (1996), 'Networked learner support', *Library Association Record*, **98**(1), January.

Line, Maurice (1974), 'The case for information officers' in Lubens, J. (ed.), *Educating the library user*, New York and London: Bowker.

Makulowich, John S. (1994), 'Tips on how to teach the Internet', *Online*, **18**(6), November/December.

Master, Nancy (1995), 'Taking the mystery out of the library: user education at UNLV's Dickinson Library', *The Reference Librarian*, 48.

Pacey, Philip (1995), 'Teaching the self-explanatory library' in *The New Review of Academic Librarianship*, 1.

Page, Mary and Kesselman, Martin (1994), 'Teaching Internet: challenges and opportunities', *Research Strategies*, **12**(3).

Scott, John F. (1994), 'Training the trainers – an introduction to teaching other people about the Internet', in *Online information 94. 18th international online meeting proceedings. London, 6–8 December 1994*, Oxford: Learned Information.

Shaikh, Thair (1996), 'On course for success in the virtual classroom', *The Times Interface*, 20 November.

Tiefel, Virginia M. (1995), 'Library user education: examining its past, projecting its future', *Library Trends*, **44**(2), Fall.

Yacci, Michael (1994), 'A grounded theory of student choice in information-rich learning environments', *Journal of Educational Multimedia and Hypermedia*, **3**(3/4).

8 Publicity and promotion

Since academic libraries largely exist to support the work of members of the educational institution, it follows that they will be best served if the library publicizes and promotes the services designed to help them. There is, however, an unwillingness in public services to dedicate large sums to marketing and, with academic libraries struggling to meet manifest demands, there is a natural reluctance towards strategies which seek to increase demand. So much so, that one prominent academic librarian (Revill 1996, p.245) has expressed a wish to 'popularise a new expression in our field – DRS, standing for "demand reduction strategies" ', as his experience at Liverpool John Moores University has been that demand simply remains high, though services may decline in quality and complaints increase. It is certainly true that librarians have to think carefully before introducing new services as it is always very difficult to withdraw them once they have begun, but it is a great strength of the academic library that it is well used and needed. To keep it that way requires a marketing strategy to 'ensure that the current users remain users, generate more enquiries/loans from existing users and attract new users' (Coote 1993, pp.338–9).

Effective performance by an academic library in any of its activities requires analysis followed by action. This is especially true of marketing. Yorke (1981, pp.2–24) has provided a helpful framework for analysis and action and I shall draw on it in what follows.

Analysis

The first area to be analysed is the environment, emphasizing those elements which affect academic institutions and their libraries. This analysis has already been covered in earlier chapters, particularly in relation to educational policy, changes in teaching and learning, and political, demographic and technological factors. Each library will, of course, need to examine its own environment, which will be strongly affected by the situation nationally.

Second, a quantitative analysis of the 'market' is needed. This should include all those who are likely 'buyers and users'. The various segments of this market need to be identified so that they can be viewed as target groups at which publicity can be aimed. Previous chapters have attempted to identify the most important groups, whether they be academic staff, support staff, researchers, external users, or students of various types who can be classified by subject, mode of attendance, special needs, nationality or other criteria.

Third, an analysis of strengths and weaknesses of an academic library must be made. A popular method is to employ a SWOT analysis to identify Strengths, Weaknesses, Opportunities and Threats. For marketing purposes academic libraries have many strengths which can be exploited. For example, they generally have a solid, reliable image and they seem likely to endure for some considerable time into the future, though their nature may change. Atkinson (1992) found the 'primary promotional factors' which make or stop people using the library are the quality of stock, the quality of services and the extent to which they meet users' needs. In the three libraries he investigated quality of stock and quality of services were clearly plus points.

Library staff, their demeanour and attitude, were also found to be important strengths in the view of users; so much so that Atkinson recommends a switch of resources from those activities which library staff view as important, such as user education and publications, to those considered important by users, with customer care training a priority. Academic libraries serve a largely captive audience about which there is plenty of documentation, increasingly in machine-readable format, which can easily be used for promotional purposes.

On the weakness side resources are now so often overstretched that availability of items has worsened. Dearing's student survey found that nearly half the students were dissatisfied with library provision (National Committee Inquiry into Higher Education 1997, p.36). As libraries move from holdings to access through information technology, availability should improve, but this is highly dependent on funds being obtainable for the changes to be made. With student numbers increasing, many academic libraries have become crowded and noisy, though funds are currently being made available for building and refurbishing, particularly in higher education (Brockhurst 1996, pp.584–5). Libraries, however, are considered to be relatively secure and safe for users, materials and equipment. Institutions are more likely therefore to locate expensive services within them. Even where full convergence has not taken place, computing facilities have frequently been placed in a building which is open and staffed for long hours, but this strength has been seriously questioned in recent years with increases in theft and vandalism:

The security of libraries presents particular problems, since inevitably security measures conflict with the demand for greater accessibility to the collections and with the librarian's primary need to encourage use of them. They conflict with the 'open door' policies which are currently fashionable and with the real and very necessary desire to make libraries welcoming and friendly places where the emphasis lies on meeting the needs of readers with the minimum of rules and regulations. (Smethurst 1991, pp.19–22)

Libraries also still have a boring and traditional image, derived largely from an emphasis on (old) books and a certain lack of creativity. This is especially the case in further education, where more students are unfamiliar with regular use of libraries. Again this could change with the impact of technology.

Opportunities at the moment seem to revolve around involvement with information technology and the way in which libraries cope with 'competitors' in the market. They range from the supply of information directly to offices and homes, to internal departments within the institution, such as media services and computing services where convergence has not taken place. Information brokers have also come on the scene where information is needed urgently and clients are prepared to pay for it.

Where a cost centre philosophy is operating, libraries have to show that their services are good value for money. As in commercial marketing, price is becoming more important as users are able to make choices in the purchase of specialized services which may not be offered 'free of charge' such as photocopying, inter-library loans, and online searches. All these opportunities can also be viewed more pessimistically as threats, and I strongly support the views of Rowley, writing about libraries and marketing, that a crucial factor in the future will be the quality of library staff: 'multi-skilled librarians with a range of management qualifications and experience in different environments should be particularly prized and staff development programmes need to offer the opportunity to develop this range of skills' (Rowley 1995, pp.24–35).

The analytical stage also requires an examination of the range of products and services which can be offered. Marketing analysts are concerned with product life cycles and these are very much in the mind of academic librarians at the present time. 'Product lifecycle theory maintains that all products or services follow distinctive patterns over time. The stages in the product lifecycle curve are Introduction, Growth, Maturity, Decline' (Elliott de Saez 1993, p.35). The book has probably reached 'maturity' and is being replaced by the new technology. The number of books published, however, shows few signs of decline. Librarians have to purchase materials in a wider range of formats and weigh the merits of one against another. Although books have not so far been replaced by electronic media, abstracting and indexing journals are being replaced in libraries by CD-ROMs and online searching. Already there has been a good deal of discussion about the product life cycle of CD-ROMs (McSean and Law 1990, pp.837–41). In the commercial world products whose life cycle is declining are withdrawn as profit margins decrease. In the public services it is less easy to withdraw services, even when little-used, and there is pressure to reach the whole market rather than any one segment, which may offer substantial growth prospects. Thus there is pressure to provide a range of materials for courses which have recruited only small numbers of students and to maintain special collections which are often unique, but take up considerable resources in their maintenance, including security, and are only used by a small number of scholars each year. There is a body of opinion which believes that such collections should be considered national assets meriting national support.

Action

A 'stair-step' approach has been popular with exponents of marketing, and is a helpful way of looking at the promotion of academic library services. Marketing communications are viewed as having a hierarchy of effects moving the customer closer to the act of purchase or use. The starting-point is awareness, followed by knowledge, then comprehension, liking, preference, conviction, purchase or use, satisfaction and, it is hoped, repeat purchase and use. The various publicity and promotion activities can be analysed in this way. For example Caswell (1985, pp.165–7) has similarly listed the major goals of an exhibition programme as education, increased use, public relations and collection development.

Another useful way of thinking about promotion with users in mind is to focus on the needs behind purchases or uses rather than what is being sold or offered. Thus customers buy nutrition (not bread), beauty (not cosmetics), warmth (not fuel). In an academic library context the needs of users might be a good mark for a piece of assessed work (not an inter-library loan), an improved contribution to a group discussion (not a book), an enjoyable learning atmosphere (not a seat in the library). Virtually every advertisement we see uses this technique, so there is no reason why it should not help the academic library seeking to increase its volume and quality of use.

Once it has been decided which services need to be promoted to which segments of the market and these services have been tailored to needs, then they have to be communicated to members of that market segment. Communication can be directed towards the group as a whole or to individual members, following the trend towards a more personal kind of marketing which includes 'approaching target prospects as individuals' (Rapp and Collins 1987) using databases and continuing to develop the relationship after sales or use. It has always been my view that librarians take insufficient interest in the use made of library materials, even those that have been used as a result of advice from the librarian. Just a brief enquiry the next time the user is seen can make all the difference, whether it takes place at a meeting, in the refectory, or on the next library visit.

Promotional methods

Libraries are able to use a wide range of promotion methods, and a whole package of measures is usually preferable to a single method. Inside the library there will be visual information such as directional signs, instructional signs and warning signs. These notices are essential elements in the provision of a 'self-explanatory' library (see Chapter 7, p.120–21) and their design (colour, quality, visual coordination) should be given expert attention. The question of how the user perceives them must always be asked; therefore experiments with active user participation are most desirable. It is too easy for library staff to become so familiar with the layout and the equipment that they forget that users may see things quite differently. Particular attention should be given to information overload caused by too many notices with no obvious prioritization. In addition, notices can easily become just part of the furniture, so changes need to be made quite frequently and, of course, information should always be kept up to date.

All academic libraries produce promotional literature of some kind, ranging from library guides to bookmarks publicizing particular services. For some libraries such production has almost become an industry, but too often the objectives and target audience for the publications are not defined and the relationship between new material available in electronic form and printed material has not been properly worked out. Use of the material is rarely monitored, so that it is difficult to assess whether it has achieved its objectives.

Despite the electronic revolution, academic libraries are still very much involved with the printed word; therefore the printed material they produce should be of a quality that sets an example to others. Unfortunately that is not always the case. The quality of the design and presentation is especially important from a public relations viewpoint, and for its contribution to readability. Manchester Metropolitan University Library has produced its own house-style manual to ensure that all material is well designed (Jordan 1995). The manual was drawn up by a professional designer and covers such areas as typeface, type size, line length, paragraphing, illustrations, abbreviations, and numbers in the text, and is consistent with the house style of its parent institution, including the use of a logo.

The quality of the writing is equally important and should always have the target audience and its knowledge and understanding in mind. This is particularly true concerning the use of library jargon.

Audiovisual guidance, enhanced by computerization, is increasingly being used to inform users and has been discussed in Chapter 7.

Well-presented exhibitions – 'displays of a significant number of items organized in such a way as to convey information to the viewer' (Caswell 1985, p.165) – can be very expensive in staff time, but users do notice them and they do indicate a certain liveliness in the library. Atkinson (1992) found that libraries that made a feature of displays were 'well regarded' by library users. Caswell's view is that 'exhibit planners should always be able to relate their show to the academic enterprise' (Caswell 1985, p.165) so that, for example, a photographic exhibition could be mounted when a class is studying the history of photography, and fine examples of nineteenth-century book illustration would enhance the study of printing. Such exhibitions have the added advantage of indicating the wider range of materials possessed by the library, thus changing the perception of users. It has also been my experience that users like to be involved with exhibitions by, for example, providing items. I well remember a very popular exhibition of home crafts which was excellent publicity for the library. Repeats of popular exhibitions and circulation among site libraries save on resources and take advantage of the fact that audiences in academic institutions differ significantly geographically and over fairly short periods of time.

Outside the library itself users need constantly to be informed and reminded about the library and its services. Eternal vigilance is required to ensure that the library is included on directional signs, maps and plans, and institutional publications such as newsletters and house magazines. It is surprising how much of this material can be erroneous where the library is concerned when written by other members of the institution (especially public relations!), though the fact that this is so reinforces the need for vigilance.

In commerce a large number of promotional techniques are used to entice potential customers, such as free samples, coupon offers, reduced prices, two for the price of one, free gifts, competitions and trading stamps. Academic libraries tend to be traditional in their approach, though some of the techniques are used on a small scale. For example, competitions are held with books or tokens as prizes, library suppliers are persuaded to give prizes for outstanding students, and fine amnesties are offered for the return of long-overdue books. Again the likely message to the user should be foremost when deciding on techniques. Prizes and competitions are usually well received and present photo-opportunities.

In spite of the pressure on academic libraries, they still need to publicize their services if users are to be made aware of the support they can receive. A systematic approach is required, consisting of a thorough analysis prior to decisions being taken on the best methods to be employed. The perception of the user must be a priority both in the analysis and the activities which follow.

References

Atkinson, Peter Jeremy (1992), *Investigation of the effectiveness of promotional activities in Polytechnic libraries*, M.Phil. thesis, Newcastle upon Tyne: Newcastle Polytechnic.

Brockhurst, Chris (1996), 'Building for the future', *Library Association Record*, **98**(11), November.

Caswell, Lucy (1985), 'Building a strategy for academic library exhibits', *College and Research Library News*, **46**(4), April.

Coote, Helen (1993), 'Marketing matters – to you, your staff, your customers . . .', *Aslib Information*, **21**(9), September.

Elliott de Saez, Eileen (1993), *Marketing concepts for libraries and information services*, London: Library Association.

Jordan, Peter (1995), *Staff management in library and information work*, 3rd edn, Aldershot: Gower.

McSean, Tony and Law, Derek (1990), 'Is CD ROM a transient technology?', *Library Association Record*, November.

National Committee of Inquiry into Higher Education (1997), *Higher education in the learning society*, London: HMSO.

Rapp, Stan and Collins, Thomas L. (1987), *Maximarketing: the new direction in advertising, promotion and marketing*, Maidenhead: McGraw-Hill.

Revill, D. H. (1996), 'Demand reduction strategies no joke' (letter), *Library Association Record*, **98**(5), May.

Rowley, J. E. (1995), 'From storekeeper to salesman: implementing the marketing concept in libraries', *Library Review*, **44**(1).

Smethurst, J. M. (1991), 'Library security: an overview', in Quinsee,

A. G. and McDonald, A. C, *Security in academic and research libraries*, Newcastle upon Tyne: University Library.

Yorke, David (1981), 'Marketing concepts and the library', in Judd, Philip M. (ed.), *Marketing the library: techniques for managing the library in hard times*, Newcastle upon Tyne: Association of Assistant Librarians.

9 The future

Information technology

Information technology inevitably dominates discussion of the future of academic librarianship. In earlier chapters its influence has been frequently discussed.

In this chapter I want to discuss major changes which are taking place as a result of technological advance, and which must be taken account of and used to the advantage of librarians and information workers if they are to take on a leadership role. Although librarians were among the earliest exponents of self-service (long before the retail trade), initial use of online information systems in academic libraries was normally through an intermediary, partly to control costs and partly because the systems were unfamiliar and user-unfriendly. Although OPAC catalogues quickly became popular among users, terminals were at first confined to the library premises. The situation now and increasingly in the future is that users will be able to search for information from outside the library, whether from desktops on campuses or from remote sites such as their own homes. The librarian's role as an intermediary will not disappear completely as library users will inevitably encounter problems during in-library searching and need help. However, with systems becoming more user-friendly and increasing pressure on academic staff to make greater use of information technology and save time, the librarian's role as an intermediary will diminish. If the new technology is to have its desired impact, a key requirement will be 'better educated end users which in turn means more librarians and support staff better prepared to give advice and guidance' (Day, Walton and Edwards 1996, p.18). Such a change of role will require careful and sensitive management if it is to succeed, since librarians who have introduced and developed electronic information services may find it hard to relinquish the intermediary role.

Academic librarians have had to work closely with computing staff in the development of information technology. In the future this will be so necessary that the distinction between the two groups of support staff will become much less clear, and new structures for support staff will become inevitable. Strategic plans submitted to the Higher Education Funding Council for England reveal that universities expect to replace lecturers with information technology, and large sums are to be spent on information technology suites and libraries with multimedia facilities (Thomson and Tysome 1996, p.1). This suggests that library buildings themselves will not become redundant, since students will still require adequate study accommodation for long hours to support resource-based learning. Moreover, academic staff still seem to appreciate the social function of the library – a place to which thay can acceptably escape, mix with others, talk to librarians and exercise serendipity, an art scarcely recognized in computerization.

Librarians should be in a strong position 'to take a leadership role in the provision of networked information. Our experience with organizing and providing access to information allows us to make substantial contributions to the development of navigational tools . . . If librarians do not take a strong leadership role, we will miss an opportunity to share our expertise in information seeking and retrieval' (Page and Kesselman 1994, p.166). This is true at international, national and local levels, and it applies not only to the development of navigational tools but also to the management of information within institutions.

It is essential that librarians analyse their situation in a systematic manner so that they can plan developments and adopt an effective leadership role. Corrall (1993) has provided a helpful list of critical factors which can be used as a checklist and which has been drawn upon in the following discussion. An effective IT infrastructure operating locally, nationally and internationally is essential, embracing 'both technical aspects – ensuring connectivity and appropriate user interfaces – and service elements, such as operator support and help desk facilities, which ideally ought to be available to coincide with opening hours for the library and PC laboratories' (Corrall 1993, p.176). From the users' point of view everything should be in reliable working order. They care little about who is responsible, but they want something done quickly when things go wrong. The major message of this book has been that the library must work with the rest of the institution if it is to realize its potential. The library's IT strategy should be developed in the context of the information strategy of the institution. Many institutions include IT development in their corporate plans; this in turn affects departments which are expected to prioritize IT in their own plans. In some cases the library has been the most forward-thinking and innovative user of IT, in which case it will be looked to for advice and leadership, especially in the early days. Where development has been fragmented and uncoordinated, the necessity for standardization and central direction has become increasingly clear.

If services are to work well, dedicated technical support is essential (Corrall 1993, p.177). Corrall states her dependence at Aston on the expertise and energy of the library's own computer officer, and my experience at Manchester Metropolitan University strongly confirms this view. At Manchester it was also felt necessary to create a new post of Information Technology Librarian, part of whose job was to liaise with computing services and to coordinate IT training.

Training

Successful use of IT is also dependent on the computer literacy of the library staff, the academic staff and the students. The education of users has been discussed in Chapter 7. The service provided by the library and the effectiveness of its user education require high-quality training of library staff. This will result initially from an analysis of the knowledge, skills and attitudes demanded of the various groups of staff. Such an analysis needs to reveal the gap between what is required for effective performance and the prevailing situation. Information is obtainable from a number of sources. Job descriptions and specifications provide a starting-point, though they are rarely up to date and will need updating through staff interviews, preferably as part of an appraisal scheme. As the information is being gathered, new staffing structures will need to be considered, since the nature of many jobs will change, and convergence with other support services offers positive benefits. Areas of overlap between library and computer staff will increase as more academic information becomes available electronically. Terminals will become multi-functional:

capable of accessing bibliographic and other databases as well as enabling information extracted from them to be manipulated and incorporated within the students' own work. When this happens, demarcation disputes between librarians who will only help students to locate the information required, and computer specialists who will only help with the programmes to process it, will be totally unacceptable in any service-orientated organisation. It is clear, however, that the attitudinal changes will not occur by themselves but will need positive encouragement and management. (Williams 1994, pp.68–9)

Although totally hybrid posts may not be the solution, an integration of some core duties in non-specialist posts increases flexibility and enables a more responsive service to be provided. With the resulting job enlargement there should eventually be greater job satisfaction and motivation if the changes are sensitively handled.

Surveys of staff can also be very helpful in developing a training strategy. A carefully administered survey should reveal feelings of inadequacy experienced by staff which can be relieved by training. It is likely that some staff will ask for training in areas where such skills will not be required in their current jobs, though the additional improvement in motivation might be a deciding factor. The main thrust of the analysis, however, should be upon the changing environment and the knowledge and skills required to provide effective services in the future. Feedback from service appraisals, user surveys and complaints by users can also be taken into account when building up a picture of training needs.

Many well-managed libraries have produced written training policies which include aims and objectives, details of those responsible for training, the various types of training available, procedures for obtaining training and methods of training evaluation. The aims should emphasize the need for staff to adapt successfully to rapid change and future developments, and spell out the importance of technological change and innovation.

Whenever change is taking place, communication and consultation with those affected is essential. Ignorance of what is happening engenders false fears and scare stories whilst honest and open discussion of the challenges involved stimulates support and encourages positive contributions from all affected.

New formats and old

The present situation with copyright, licensing and leasing arrangements is 'highly complex with suppliers offering a multiplicity of different terms and conditions ... products that initially seem to provide a cost-effective solution can become very expensive when networked; pressure must be brought to bear on suppliers to adopt a more uniform approach' (Corrall 1993, p.176).

Brown (1993, pp.27–66) did not believe that traditional publishers were geared up for forays into electronic publishing, but significant progress has been made, due, to a considerable extent, to the Pilot Site Licence Initiative (PSLI) and the Electronic Libraries (e Lib) research programmes. Hitchcock, Carr and Hall (1997, p.298) have produced figures which show that approximately 1300 'UK' journals were available by 1997 and around 3200 are projected for 1998/99 when most major journals should be available online. This is seen as 'a massive switch by publishers to embrace the idea of delivery of journals in electronic form. It is not a switch to paperless publishing because almost universally these e-journals are based on page-by-page replicas of the paper originals' (Hitchcock, Carr and Hall 1997, p.285). In the future we are likely to see greater innovation making use of the possibilities of the network.

Librarians have to wrestle with this constantly changing environment at a time when funding is under great pressure. Thus Corrall (1993, p.176) makes the point that the transition from print to electronic sources can be eased by running the two modes in parallel and evaluating the different systems, but the trend towards cost centres and formula funding makes the possibility of operating in this way unlikely. Sylvia and Lesher (1994, pp.59–64) describe a situation with which many academic librarians will be familiar today as they face 'the dual problems of increasing costs and the desire to utilize new and ever-changing technologies'. In a very practical way they describe the criteria used in making decisions about keeping or cancelling printed indexes versus electronic formats. The first criterion is price, and this includes costs of subscription and other charges such as phone and database use costs, space, preservation, replacement of lost pages or volumes, labour costs in ordering, receiving, marking up and updating the library's database. Costs of equipment, of training library staff and users, and time spent updating software also have to be taken into account.

Second, ease of access needs to be considered. Electronic indexes are potentially much easier to use and provide greatly improved searching capabilities, although browsing is more difficult and such indexes depend on reliable equipment.

Third, use has to be assessed, for example, the current use of a paper index, especially if covered by a CD-ROM or online database. The impact of electronic searching on other areas of the library needs to be monitored and reviewed. A number of articles cited by Sylvia and Lesher reported a drop in online searching after the introduction of CD-ROM, whilst other libraries have experienced increases in journal subscription requests and inter-library loan activity.

The actual quality of the indexing and the content has to be taken into account since the CD-ROM or online database may not be an exact replacement for the paper index.

Ownership is also seen by Sylvia and Lesher as an important factor to consider. There are always worries about electronic services going out of business, leaving the library without a paper back-up, and about deterioration of formats such as CD-ROM.

Equipment required to access material is expensive, frequently needs replacing as technology progresses, and incurs heavy maintenance costs. Networked databases require higher subscriptions and subsidized database services such as BIDS are likely to become more expensive. When computers first made their impact on libraries, especially with the automation of housekeeping routines, resource managers may often have expected financial savings as machines took over the work of humans. In further and higher education the real result has been that automation has enabled institutions to cope with great increases in demand without increases in staffing, and now they are able to provide a much wider range of services, which should improve the quality of work performed by academic staff and students, simultaneously saving them time when searching for information. Gorman (1991, p.5) is firmly of the view that libraries are underfunded and that innovation and the use of technology for innovation are seen, by some, as ways to make up for underfunding. 'Innovation and technology improve the cost/efficiency ratio by raising the efficiency *not* by lowering the cost.'

Although electronic services have become a major feature of most academic libraries, printed materials still dominate and audiovisual formats, particularly videotapes, have become important elements.

New technologies do not always *abolish* previous technologies. People still go to concerts despite the advanced state of to-day's recording/playing; television has killed neither the radio nor the book. New technologies should be seen as doing what they always do – supplementing and enhancing old technologies. (Gorman 1991, p.6)

Some formats, such as microforms, films, and various video formats have either reached the end of their product life for library purposes or are moving in that direction. So far the development of the electronic journal has been slow. The librarian of today has to get the mix right in an ever-changing environment.

Other areas of change

The future will see continuing change in many areas, other than information technology, which will affect academic libraries, though it is difficult to view any without some reference to the contribution of information technology.

The search for changes in course design and teaching methods will continue as institutions wrestle with the task of providing effective but more efficient tuition as student numbers increase and the student body becomes more heterogeneous. Recent pressure for easier access for those with poor pre-entry qualifications, and for the adoption of inclusive learning policies to match the specific learning needs and styles of students with learning difficulties/disabilities, will present formidable challenges to librarians at a time when reductions in students' financial support will bring further decline in their book purchasing.

Unfortunately increases in theft and vandalism seem unlikely to abate as students struggle financially, and pressure needs to be brought on institutions to take anti-social behaviour more seriously than they do at present.

Quality provision will continue to be sought by the quality assurance agencies and it is hoped that they will become less bureaucratic and will give greater prominence to library and learning resource provision. An area of quality which needs seriously to be addressed is customer service, which will be under severe pressure in coping with the changes taking place. Here especially a social action approach is required and this will only be satisfactory if librarians involve themselves with users and user groups, both formally and informally. Librarians need to gain the trust of users, and this may require further subject qualifications, improved publicity and frequent demonstrations of worth.

High-quality user education is a priority for both students and academic staff, with an emphasis on efficient information seeking through information technology.

The Dearing Report was eager to point out that collaboration between institutions should not be discouraged:

At the heart of our vision of higher education is the freestanding institution, which offers teaching to the highest level in an environment of scholarship and independent enquiry. But, collectively and individually, these institutions are becoming ever more central to the economic wellbeing of the nation, localities and individuals. There is a growing bond of interdependence, in which each is looking for much from the other. That interdependence needs to be more clearly recognised by all the participants. (National Committee of Inquiry into Higher Education 1997, p.11)

Along with the contribution of information technology, such collaboration could be seen as the way forward for academic libraries in coping with the demands of the future. The Consortium of Academic Libraries in Manchester and the M25 Consortium of Higher Education in London have recently shown what can be achieved through such activities as joint access arrangements, cooperative purchase, document delivery services and staff training.

The situation in further and higher education is changing every day and libraries are struggling to respond, but respond they must if they are to maintain their position at the heart of the educational enterprise. I have attempted in this book to describe changes which are taking place and suggest priorities for immediate action, since the future has already begun. Academic librarians must fight for their own futures or they will be left in the past.

References

Brown, David (1993), 'Present status of electronic publishing within the UK publishing industry' in *Libraries and IT: working papers of the Information Technology Sub-committee of the HEFCs' Libraries Review*, Bristol: UKOLN.

Corrall, Sheila (1993), 'ADONIS at Aston: introducing electronic document delivery in the networked library' in *Libraries and IT: working papers of the Information Technology Sub-committee of the HEFCs' Libraries Review*, Bristol: UKOLN.

Day, Joan M., Walton, Graham and Edwards, Catherine (1996), 'The human face of change', *Library Technology*, **1**(1), February.

Gorman, Michael (1991), 'The academic library in the year 2001: dream or nightmare or something in between?', *Journal of Academic Librarianship*, **17**(1), March.

Hitchcock, Steve, Carr, Leslie and Hall, Wendy (1997), 'Web journals publishing: a UK perspective', *Serials*, **10**(3), November.

National Committee of Inquiry into Higher Education (1997), *Higher education in the learning society: report of the National Committee* (The Dearing Report), London: HMSO.

Page, Mary and Kesselman, Martin (1994), 'Teaching the Internet: challenges and opportunities', *Research Strategies*, **12**(3), Summer.

Sylvia, Margaret and Lesher, Marcella (1994), 'Making hard choices: cancelling print indexes', *Online*, 63, January.

Thomson, Alan and Tysome, Tony (1996), 'Lecturers frozen out', *The Times Higher Education Supplement*, 1255, 22 November 1996.

Williams, A. G. (1994), 'Where are we going? the development of convergence between university libraries and computing services', in Harris, Colin (ed.), *The new university library: issues for the '90s and beyond*, London: Taylor Graham.

Index

155